# YHVH's Three Angels' Messages for the Christian Church

Donald Werner
04/2/2023

# **Copyright**

YHVH's Three Angels' Messages for the Christian Church
Copyright © 2023 Donald Werner. All rights reserved.
ISBN #: 978-1-312-71605-6
Published by Donald Werner

Scripture taken from the New King James Version®. Copyright © 1982 by Thomas Nelson. Used by permission. All rights reserved. All Scriptures, unless otherwise marked are from the NKJV.

Scriptures taken from the Holy Bible, New International Version®, NIV®. Copyright © 1973, 1978, 1984, 2011 by Biblica, Inc.™ Used by permission of Zondervan. All rights reserved

Scriptures taken from the Holy Bible, English Standard Version® ESV® Bible (The Holy Bible, English Standard Version®), copyright © 2001 by Crossway, a publishing ministry of Good News Publishers. Used by permission. All rights reserved.

Scriptures taken from the New American Standard Bible (NASB)
Copyright © 1960, 1962, 1963, 1968, 1971, 1972, 1973, 1975, 1977, 1995 by The Lockman Foundation

All scripture emphases, bolding, underlining, italics and parenthetical notes are mine.

Please note, with concerns of violating the Second Commandment, using God's name in vain, His sacred name (YHVH) was removed from the printed Bibles and substituted with the title 'the LORD'. I have restored God's sacred name of God, "YHVH", back into the Scriptures which I quote, where it had been replace by the translators with the phrase "the LORD". I felt that was necessary to get the true understanding of the Scriptures. Exodus 3:15, **"Moreover God said to Moses, "Thus you shall say to the children of Israel: 'YHVH God of your fathers, the God of Abraham, the God of Isaac, and the God of Jacob, has sent me to you. This is My name forever, and this is My memorial to all generations.'."**

| | |
|---|---|
| **Copyright** | 2 |
| **THE PREFACE** | 5 |
| **THE INTRODUCTION** | 6 |
| **CHAPTER 1 – THE BOOK OF THE REVELATION** | 8 |
| THE SIGNIFICANCE OF THE BOOK OF THE REVELATION | 8 |
| WHY THE BOOK OF THE REVELATION? | 8 |
| KEY DEFINITIONS TO UNDERSTAND | 9 |
| GOD'S NAME | 9 |
| THE TWO TYPES OF SINNERS | 11 |
| PRESUMPTUOUS SINNERS MUST REPENT | 13 |
| SAVED BY GRACE | 14 |
| TRUE REPENTANCE | 15 |
| NO NEW COVENANT | 17 |
| IS JESUS GOD? | 21 |
| **CHAPTER 2 – REVELATION'S SEVEN CHURCHES** | 23 |
| REVELATION CHAPTER 2-3 - LETTERS TO THE SEVEN CHURCHES | 23 |
| THE MESSAGES TO THE SEVEN CHURCHES; | 24 |
| THE SYNAGOGUE OF SATAN | 28 |
| ARE WE LAODICEA TODAY? | 37 |
| NOT MY CHURCH | 39 |
| CONCLUSION | 42 |
| SUMMARY OF CHURCH MESSAGES | 44 |
| PAUL'S CHURCHES? | 45 |
| **CHAPTER 3 – SIX SEALS AND FOUR HORSES** | 46 |
| THE FOUR HORSES OF THE APOCALYPSE | 46 |
| THE DEATH OF CHRISTIANITY | 47 |
| **CONCLUSION** | 47 |
| **CHAPTER 4 – THE THREE ANGEL'S MESSAGES** | 48 |
| REVELATION CHAPTER 14 | 48 |
| THE CHRISTIAN CHURCH IS BABYLON | 49 |
| THE REDEEMED – HOW TO BE ONE OF THEM… | 50 |
| THE REDEEMED SING A NEW SONG UNTO YHVH | 55 |
| WHAT YHVH OUR GOD WANTS OF US IS A 'NEW SONG'. | 55 |
| CLOSING ARGUMENTS | 56 |

| | |
|---|---|
| THE FIRST ANGEL'S MESSAGE - THE EVERLASTING GOSPEL | 56 |
| WHAT IS WORSHIP? | 61 |
| TRUE WORSHIP | 61 |
| TWO REASONS TO OBEY THE EVERLASTING GOSPEL; | 63 |
| NOT FOR CHRISTIANS | 64 |
| A COUNTERFEIT GOSPEL? | 64 |
| WHAT IS THE GOSPEL IN TODAY'S CHRISTIAN CHURCHES? | 65 |
| THE SECOND ANGEL'S MESSAGE – A WARNING | 67 |
| THE THIRD ANGEL'S MESSAGE – DON'T WORSHIP THE BEAST | 68 |
| **NO PERFECT OBEDIENCE FOR THE REDEEMED SAINTS** | **71** |
| ARE YOU PREFECT? | 71 |
| TWO TYPES OF CHRISTIANS | 72 |
| WHAT IS THE MAIN MESSAGE IN THE BOOK OF THE REVELATION? | 74 |
| **CHAPTER 5 – PAUL** | **75** |
| PAUL THE DECEIVER | 75 |
| WHY ARE PAUL'S TEACHINGS CONTRARY TO JESUS' TEACHINGS? | 75 |
| I COULD HAVE DONE BETTER THAN ADAM AND EVE | 77 |
| JESUS SAID WATCH OUT FOR THE TEACHINGS OF THE PHARISEES | 78 |
| JESUS SAID THE PHARISEES WERE LAWLESS | 78 |
| A SMALL SECT OF THE PHARISEES WERE NOT LAWLESS | 81 |
| WHY WERE PAUL AND MOST OF THE PHARISEES LAWLESS? | 82 |
| PAUL'S IDEA FOR SALVATION | 86 |
| WHY WAS THE PHARISEES' WORSHIP IN VAIN? | 87 |
| DO WE WORSHIP IN VAIN? | 88 |
| WAS PAUL AN APOSTATE? | 89 |
| PAUL'S TEACHINGS IN CONTRAST TO JESUS' TEACHINGS | 91 |
| WHO ARE THESE FALSE PROPHETS? | 92 |
| THE EARLY CHURCH WASN'T LAWLESS | 93 |
| BY FOLLOWING PAUL'S TEACHINGS WE BECOME LAWLESS | 93 |
| WAS PAUL REBUKED BY THE TRUE APOSTLES? | 94 |
| A LYING SPIRIT? | 96 |
| "FAITH OF JESUS" VS. "FAITH IN JESUS" | 97 |
| PREDICTED APOSTASY FROM JESUS' TEACHINGS | 98 |
| THE BOOK OF THE REVELATION IS ANTI-PAUL | 99 |
| CHAPTER CONCLUSION | 99 |

# THE PREFACE

The Three Angels' Messages are only directed to those in the Christian Church, of to every nation, tribe, tongue, and people, for only Christians will read that Book. Those messages tell those in the Church why and how they must 'get out' of the Christian Church and what they must do to be among the redeemed. Why would God send His angels to deliver such a message? That's what this book is all about.

The Book of the Revelation is Yahoveh (YHVH) God's last 'written' message to mankind. YHVH's final message was given to His anointed Prophet Jesus who then he passed it onto the Apostle John – who penned it (Revelation 1:1). That makes this Book an extremely important book, because it is YHVH's final revelation for mankind, Jesus' last recorded words and John's last written words. Being YHVH God's final message means it's His final words of any subject that is addressed in His last revelation – and His revelation addresses many topics: the Gospel, the law, the Church, Babylon, the judgment, redemption, condemnation, the Beast, his image, his mark, seal of God, repentance, worship, etc.

The Book of the Revelation is like a capstone on a structure, or the frosting on a cake, because it contains: God's last warnings, His last instructions and His final Judgment. In that Book He tells us: what went wrong with the 'Christian Church' and why it became known as 'Babylon the Great'. God then gives us three message delivered by His messengers (angels) and that includes the way of salvation for all people, Everlasting Gospel, warnings about who we worship and a warning to get out of Babylon before the plagues start. In this book we also learn what happens to those who stay in Babylon the Great.

Revelation Chapter 14 the key to the understanding of the Book of the Revelation. Within Chapter 14 not only do we learn how to be one of the redeemed, and we also receive the Everlasting Gospel, within the first angels' Message. These messages are basically ignored by most the Christian Church, and even when they consider them they get it wrong – because the proper understanding of those message is not compatible with the doctrines and the creeds of the Christian Church.

As we study we must pay particular attention to Jesus' words, for they are the words of YHVH God (John 12:49, 14:10), and Jesus said that he is to be our only teacher (Matthew 23:10) and that means he will teach us all we need to know with regards to salvation and the issues he spoke about. If we abide in Jesus' words without being derailed by some false prophet, we will be among the redeemed (Revelation 14:1-4, 22:7), for his words alone are the words of eternal life (John 6:68). He said that if we kept His words we will avoid eternal death (John 8:51) and receive eternal life (Matthew 7:24-27, John 10:27-28, 15:10). If we accept him as our only teacher we will know the truth which will set us free us free from the damning deceptions Jesus warned us about (John 8:32). And Jesus said it is by his words that we will judged (John 12:48-49).

That being the last book written in the New Testament era, unlike other New Testament books, it was not written to convince the Jews that Jesus is the Messiah and it was not written to convert pagans to worship the true God. This book was written to the already established and future Christian Church, and it must be understood in that context. The Book of Revelation is a Book to the Christian Church, a book of warnings, rebukes, encouragement, and direction. And we must grasp what it is telling us.

End

## THE INTRODUCTION

As background material which is needed to understand Chapter 14 and the Three Angel's Messages, we will take a quick look at the Seven Churches in Chapter 2 and 3 and then the Four Horses in Chapter 6. In those sections we will learn what went wrong with the Christian Church.

The Seven Churches and the Four Horses, in the Book of the Revelation, each chronicle how the Christian Church has fallen from its perfect inception, to its current and final state of corruption and death. After explaining all of that, God then calls His people out of today's corrupt lukewarm Christian Church, which is then referred to as "Babylon the Great". Those who stay in "Babylon the Great" will receive, or earn, the Mark of the Beast and receive 'her plagues'. Those who do come out of 'Babylon the Great' are redeemed and will enter the New Jerusalem, with the saints of God.

God's message, which we can gleam from the seven letters to the Seven Churches will tell us all we need to know about these Churches, and clearly these churches are not leading us into the Narrow way of salvation – but rather on the Broad way of destruction. And that's why the Three Angels' Messages are needed. God is sends three angels, each one with a message to tell Christians exactly what they must do to be one of the 144,000 redeemed.

When Jesus referred to the Christian Church as 'Babylon the Great', he wasn't talking about some future corrupt version of the Christian Church or a nation. Since the Christian Church became corrupt, shortly after its inception, it became 'Babylon on the Great'. The Seven Letters were for the people in every Christian Church, from then until today, Jesus repeatedly said, 'he who has an ear, let him hear'. I will show you just how spiritually corrupt the Christian Church is, and has been since the time of Paul.

In this book I will share with you the Biblical truths which have been set aside by the Christian Church, in favor of their own Church creeds, doctrines and traditions. Setting aside those Biblical truth has caused the once pure morally white Christian Church to become lawless, idolatrous, spiritually dead, and lukewarm in their relationship with God, and their moral behavior, thus earning themselves the title 'Babylon the Great'.

Blessings as you study,
Donald Werner, dxwerne@yahoo.com

## CHAPTER 1 – THE BOOK OF THE REVELATION

## THE SIGNIFICANCE OF THE BOOK OF THE REVELATION

The Book of the Revelation was given to mankind around the end of the First Century and it was received and written by the Apostle John. It is significant to note that it was received and written decades after all of Paul's letters were written and circulated, Paul was already dead, and all of four Gospels had already been written. It seems that God had some more He wanted us to know: more warnings, more encouragements, more rebukes, and more instructions. This revelation by God covers past, current and future events and is both a warning to those on the Broad path leading to destruction as well as hope and encouragement for those on the Narrow way leading to life.

## WHY THE BOOK OF THE REVELATION?

If I could have just one book in the New Testament, it would be the Book of the Revelation. Let me explain why.

This is a key book to understand God and God's will for mankind, for it is God's final book, His final message to mankind. If you were to write your children your last message before you went on a long journey, knowing that they would only see you if and when they came to you; what would you write? I would recap all most important things they needed to know, and all they needed to know to find their way to me when it was time for them to go. I would give them encouragement as well as warnings of all the dangers, pitfalls, and snares on their way. That's how I see the Book of the Revelation. It's God's directions to His kingdom, like a roadmap, or GPS so that we may enter by the gates and eat from the tree of life.

If you remember from reading the Gospels, Jesus had many discussions and arguments with the religious leaders, but the argument would end when Jesus would say, "**it is written**" or "**have you not read...**". Jesus would quote the Scripture, which was the greatest authority available, and that ended all arguments, for they couldn't argue with the Scriptures. In the same manner, the book of the Revelation is God's final word to settle issues that are unresolved, or things that needed to be stressed, or things that have not yet been revealed, things misunderstood, or things that needed more clarification on what the rest of the Scriptures provided. Such as; Jesus in the Gospel tells us to keep God's 'law and the Prophets' until heaven and earth pass away, yet, Paul says the law is dead, Old Covenant, and he give us 35 other reasons was we don't need to keep God's law. Who is right and who is wrong? We can go to God's final word on the subject to find the answers we need. To understand why Paul's message one of lawlessness see the Chapter on Paul.

Paul told us that we didn't need to keep YHVH's laws – but he's just one witness. Jesus (speaking YHVH's words with YHVH's authority (John 12:49, 14:10), and his apostles each told us that we need to keep YHVH's law and the

Prophets (That's three or more witnesses: YHVH, Jesus and the Apostles). Jesus said in Matthew 18:16, "...'by the mouth of two or three witnesses every word may be established."

I suspect one reason that God provided the Book of the Revelation is to counteract the lawless messages in Paul's epistles that has permeated every Christian Church. And thus, the need for the Three Angels' Messages is **"to those who dwell on the earth—to every nation, tribe, tongue, and people"** (Revelation 14:6). They all need it because all the world is deceived and follow the beast' (Revelation 12:9, 13:3).

The test for all Christians is that they are forced to choose between Jesus' words and Paul's words. That is our internal battle of Armageddon, and that is our wrestling with God.

YHVH God's ultimate goal is to have redeemable people, so that they may be fit to enter YHVH God's eternal kingdom as true worshipers of YHVH God. This is YHVH God's ultimate goal within the Scriptures and of this Book of the Revelation as well.

## KEY DEFINITIONS TO UNDERSTAND

Before we even get into the Book of the Revelation's Three Angels' Messages, there are a few key definitions that we will find useful in our study. Understanding these few concepts and terms will help us understand, not just the Book of the Revelation, but the Scriptures in general.

## GOD'S NAME

Throughout the Old Testament Hebrew Scriptures we find God's Sacred name written in four Hebrew letters, which are translated into the English letters YHVH or sometimes YHWH. The ancient Hebrew didn't have vowels, so the vowels had to be supplied by the reader. So, the pronouncement of God's name depends on the vowels added. Many people believe that the name should be pronounced Yahoveh, others say Yahweh, others say Jehoveh, and there are still other pronunciations. We can't be certain how the ancient Hebrews pronounced it, so we must all pronounce it as we are convicted. But pronounce His name we must, for we are told to call on YHVH God by name to in praise, worship and thanksgiving. Just for example, here are a few of the many verses which tell us to call on God by His Name;

Isaiah 52:6 – **"Therefore My people shall know My name; therefore they shall know in that day that I am He who speaks: 'Behold, it is I.' "**

Psalm 145:21, **"My mouth shall speak the praise of YHVH, and all flesh shall bless His holy name forever and ever."**

2Samuel 22:10, **"Therefore I will give thanks to You, O YHVH, among the Gentiles, And sing praises to Your name."**

Psalm 7:17, **"I will praise YHVH according to His righteousness, And will sing praise to the name of YHVH Most High."**

Psalm 29:2, **"Give unto YHVH the glory due to His name; worship YHVH in the beauty of holiness."**

Psalm 86:9, **"All nations whom You have made shall come and worship before You, O YHVH, and shall glorify Your name."**

Unfortunately you won't find the name 'YHVH' in most Bibles, because that name is holy and must only be used in reverence. So, the publishers of the Bibles replaced the sacred name 'YHVH' with the title 'LORD' or 'the LORD' in all caps. And, unfortunately, that substitution has caused confusion to those who don't know about it. And it has caused many people to not even know God's name. Not knowing God's name is a problem because God has given us many instructions to call on Him by name in prayer, praise, worship, and thanksgiving. In the Old Testament verses which I quote in the book, I will restore YHVH's name.

I believe that many people don't know about the substitution and when they read 'LORD' in the Scriptures they aren't really sure who 'lord' is, since 'lord' is a common title used to refer to people as well as gods. Perhaps some people will assume it refers to God, but will they understand that it is speaking of a specific God, YHVH God? So, not understanding this substitution can lead to confusion. For instance, we read in the New Testament, **"For whoever calls on the name of the Lord shall be saved."** So many people believe 'Lord is Jesus' and they call on him to be saved. But that's not true, for that verse is a direct quote from the Old Testament, and if we read Joel 2:32 in the English version we will read, **"For whoever calls on the name of the LORD shall be saved."** But the original Hebrew text didn't say, 'the LORD', it said YHVH. **For "whoever calls on the name of YHVH shall be saved."**

According to the Scriptures, such as Deuteronomy 32:8, Isaiah 63:16, 64:8 and 1Chronicles 29:10, YHVH God is also known as 'Our Father'. It was to 'Our Father' that Jesus prayed (John 17:1, Matthew 26:36) and told us to pray to (Matthew 6:9-13). Jesus referred to the Father as his 'God and his Father' (John 20:17). Jesus worshiped YHVH God, Our Father (John 4:22-23) and told us to do the same (Matthew 4:10).

Within the verses I quote in this book, I will replace the phrase 'the LORD', by restoring it back to 'YHVH' as it was in the original Hebrew.

## THE TWO TYPES OF SINNERS

In the Bible we find two types of sinners, we find the 'unintentional sinner' who commits 'unintentional sins', and the intentional sinner, or the 'presumptuous sinner', commits intentional sins. And since we are all sinners, so we all fit into one of these two types; unintentional or presumptuous. In the end, unintentional sinners are saved and presumptuous are lost, we need to know the difference, and know what type of sinner we are.

These Biblical concepts and definitions which, after 70 years as a Christian, I have never heard some explain the two types of sinners from the pulpit, or the many Bible studies I have attended, nor have I heard these during my years at the theological seminary. For most of the Christian community sin is not an issue, they will tell us to just believe in Jesus.

## PRESUMPTUOUS SINNER

Numbers 15:30 **'But the person who does *anything* presumptuously, *whether he is* native-born *(Jew)* or a stranger *(Christian)*, that one brings reproach on YHVH, and he shall be cut off from among his people."** Presumptuous sinners have rejected one or more of God's laws which they then freely violates them. They don't even consider it to be a sin to violate the 'set aside' or 'obsolete' law(s), so don't feel guilt, or the need to repent, and therefore they receive no forgiveness, and no atonement is made for them, and they are eternally lost – unless they truly repent. The calls to repentance in this Book and in the Gospels are for the presumptuous sinners. But yet, until they come to some greater knowledge of the truth, they will not repent. When the Bible speaks about 'sinners' or the 'wicked' it is referring to presumptuous sinners.

The plagues in the Book of the Revelation are designed to get those presumptuous sinners to repent. During the course of the plagues, we hear the phrase, 'yet, they did not repent'. And then the next plague is released.

A 'presumptuous sinner' is one who knows God's law(s), but has been deceived into presumptuously believing that God's law(s) are not for them. They have been told that God's laws are obsolete, out-of-date, nailed to the cross, we don't need them anymore and therefore they presume that there will be no eternal consequences for breaking them. And thus, they presume it's not a sin to violate those obsolete law(s), so they feel no guilt, godly sorrow or remorse and they presume there is no need to ever repent. Numbers 15:30 tells us that presumptuous sinners shall be 'cut off from among God's people', or cut off of the covenant with YHVH. There's no sacrifice or atonement made for presumptuous sinners. The Bible also calls presumptuous sinners those who 'practice lawlessness', 'the wicked', 'unrighteous', 'workers of iniquity' or 'the lawless' because the reject God's law(s), and their sin is often called 'iniquity'. Different translations use different names.

Hebrews 10:26, **"For if we sin willfully after we have received the knowledge of the truth, there no longer remains a sacrifice for sins"**. Hebrews 10:26 speaks about presumptuous sinners, for whom there is no atonement possible, not even Jesus' blood – until they come to the knowledge of truth and truly repent.

## UNINTENTIONAL SINNER

We read about unintentional sinners in Leviticus 4:27-28 , **'If anyone of the common people sins unintentionally by doing something against any of the commandments of YHVH in anything which ought not to be done, and is guilty, 28 or if his sin which he has committed comes to his knowledge, then he shall bring as his offering a kid of the goats, a female without blemish, for his sin which he has committed."** 'Unintentionally' doesn't necessarily mean that a person sins accidentally, that's not generally what they are doing – although that can happen as well. Unintentional sinning generally happens when a person who is convicted to keep God's law is overcome by temptation, in a moment of weakness, temporarily deceived, or has caved in to some pressure – against their better understanding. Unintentional sinners try to keep God's laws, but they too fail, but they then feel godly sorrow, guilt, remorse and they repent. They are the 'saints' of God.

The true determiner as to what type of sinner as person is if they repent, then it was an unintentional sinner – because presumptuous sinners committing intentional sins and they do not repent.

Because of their repentance, the unintentional sinner is forgiven, justified, made white as snow and atonement is made for them and they are saved.

Since we are all sinners, we all have to fit in one of these two categories – we are either saved unintentional sinners who repent, or we are condemned presumptuous sinners who will not repent. We read about both types of sinners again in Proverbs 24:16 (NKJV), **"For a righteous *man* may fall seven times and rise again, but the wicked shall fall by calamity."** The **'righteous'** are the unintentional sinners who fall into sin often (seven times), but they repent and are restored and still called "righteous". The **'wicked'** are the presumptuous sinners who fall into sin and never recover, because they will not repent, but have fallen to their own destruction, or 'calamity'.

So the 'righteous', the 'saints of God' or the 'redeemed' are not holy people who never sin, they don't exist. The righteous saints of God are the repented and forgiven sinners. It was to the presumptuous sinner that YHVH

God sent Jesus to seek and save. Matthew 9:13, **"...For I did not come to call the righteous, but sinners, to repentance."** If they don't repent, they will receive the 'Mark of the Beast'. But, those who truly repent will have the 'seal of YHVH' written on (in) their foreheads because a repentant sinner keeps the commandments of YHVH God, and YHVH God's First Commandment tells us to worship YHVH alone (Exodus 20:2-3. **"I am YHVH your God, who brought you out of the land of Egypt, out of the house of bondage; you shall have no other gods before Me"**).

It is important to understand that presumptuous sinners, or those who practice lawlessness, are often nice church going people. Practicing lawlessness doesn't mean that they are completely evil and sin every chance they get. They may be good neighbors and good people, and they may even keep most of God's commandments and laws, perhaps 99%. But by intentionally rejecting even one of God's laws or commandments, they have spurned God's Divine authority. They have looked God in the eye and said, 'No, I don't accept that law'. Any law that they have rejected and set aside or simply ignored, they will violate it and not even consider it to be a sin, and so they will never repent. Thus the very nice church going person will be condemned with those who 'practice lawlessness' to the fiery furnace (Matthew 13:41-42) with the good Christians in Matthew 7:22-23 who even called Jesus, 'Lord, Lord' and did many good Christian things but were condemned for 'practicing lawlessness'. Matthew 7:22-23, **"Many will say to Me in that day, 'Lord, Lord, have we not prophesied in Your name, cast out demons in Your name, and done many wonders in Your name?' 23 And then I will declare to them, 'I never knew you; depart from Me, you who practice lawlessness!'** Those are presumptuous sinners.

Being "born again" could be defined as the process of moving from being an unsaved presumptuous sinner who feels no need to repent, to becoming a saved unintentional sinner, who feels guilt, shame and godly sorrow whenever they sin, and then they repent.

Now, with this understanding of sins and sinners, you will have a better understanding of the Scriptures. We must be on guard that we don't fall into the presumptuous sinner category.

## PRESUMPTUOUS SINNERS MUST REPENT

God and Jesus wasted no efforts in calling presumptuous sinners to repentance, and the Book of the Revelation is no exception, the call to repentance and overcome sin related issues is common in that Book. Although we will see at some point during the judgments when there are no more calls to repentance, for then it will be too late. In Revelation 15:2 we read about presumptuous sinners who have repented. The word 'repent' is used for the last time in 16:11, when the bowls are being poured out. The bowl and the plagues are in effort to get sinners to repent.

So, presumptuous sinners are condemned because they have violated God's laws and will not repent. I know what some people are now asking; but. aren't we saved by grace apart from God's law? If so, do we really need to repent.

## **SAVED BY GRACE**

Yes, all people who are saved are only saved by God's saving grace. But we must understand, who is it that will receive God's saving grace?

Maybe we should define 'grace'? Here's a definition that makes perfect sense and it helps the Scriptures become clearer; another word for 'grace' is 'favor'. We show favor (grace) to those whom we love, to them we give forgiveness, mercy, patience, pardon, and kindness, God too shows 'grace' or 'favor' to those whom He loves, giving them forgiveness, mercy, patience, pardon and kindness. Jeremiah 31:20b, **"Therefore My heart yearns for him; I will surely have mercy on him, says YHVH."** God has mercy (favor or grace) only on those whom He loves.

And while God loves the whole world, He doesn't love everyone with the type of love that will merit God's saving grace. If God did love everyone with that type of love, then everyone would be saved, and we know that's not the case. God does have a special love for some people, and the Scriptures tell us how to get God to love us with that type of special love; I printed two of the verses below giving us the only formula in the Scriptures to gain God's special saving love which will receive His saving grace (mercy). In Exodus 20:6 YHVH God said, **"but showing mercy** (grace or loving kindness) **to thousands of generations, to those who love Me and keep My commandments."** And in John 14:21 Jesus said, **"He who has My commandments and keeps them, it is he who loves Me. And he who loves Me will be loved by My Father, and I will love him and manifest Myself to him."** The Scriptures tell us that God has a special love for those who 'love Him and keeps His commandments'. We read in Psalm 11:7, **"For YHVH is righteous, He loves righteousness…"** Psalm 146:8, **"… YHVH loves the righteous."** Why would God have a special love for the righteous who keep His commandments? Why would they alone receive His favor, or saving grace? (Remember that the righteous are sinners who have repented.)

Not only does God love those who love Him and keep His commandments, showing them grace, favor and mercy, but Exodus 20:5 tells us that YHVH considers those who will not keep His commandments to 'hate' Him.

God's grace, mercy and salvation are not simply merited by the mechanical keeping of His commands. However, when a person willingly submits to God's Divine authority, they are glorifying Him, displaying a love for God, reverence for Him, a fearful respect of Him and a true faith in Him and His word. To obey YHVH God is to honor Him and it is also an act of worship. And that is the type of person that God loves and seeks for His kingdom (John 4:23). Those who "love God and keep His commandments" are displaying the character God is looking for to fill His eternal kingdom. The rich young rule wanted to know how to inherit eternal life, and Jesus told him. Mark 10:19-21, **"You know the commandments: ...' "And he answered and said to him, "Teacher, all these things I have kept from my youth." Then Jesus, looking at him, loved him ... "**. The person who loves God and keeps His commandments is loved by God and if he/she remains in that relationship with God they will receive His saving grace, favor, mercy at judgment time.

However, those who practice lawlessness (presumptuous sinner) and will not keep God's commandments, but ignores them and sets them aside, they are rejecting God's Divine authority and that greatly dishonors Him. By their setting aside, rejecting or ignoring His laws, they are showing a lack of love for God, a lack of a respectful fear, a lack of reverence, and a lack of faith in Him and His word. They have obviously placed another authority over and above God's Divine authority. God is not pleased with such a person, and they will not merit God's love, favor or saving grace. It was to that type of person that Jesus and John the Baptizer said; **"Repent for the kingdom of God is at hand"**. In saying that, Jesus was warning sinners that they needed to repent to be welcomed into the Kingdom of God. Why must one repent before they are welcomed into God's kingdom? What is true repentance?

## **TRUE REPENTANCE**

YHVH God told us to keep His laws, and Jesus told us to keep YHVH's laws. YHVH should be our greatest authority and we should submit to His authority and obey Him. And if we submitted to Jesus, we would be submitting to YHVH because that's what he told us to do. However, if we take the advice of some lawless authority which tells us that we don't need to keep YHVH's law(s), we will set aside YHVH's law(s) and violate them. That's exactly what happened in the Garden of Eden when the serpent beast convinced Eve that she didn't need to submit to YHVH's Divine authority and could be her own god and decide for herself what is 'good and evil'.

So, it's not enough to just feel bad about our sin, and feel bad about those we hurt, and then try not to do it again. True repentance has to involve a humbling of self, or crucifying of self, and a heartfelt recommitment to make YHVH our supreme authority. Jesus gave us that process in Matthew 16:24, **"Then Jesus said to His disciples, "If anyone desires to come after Me, let him deny himself, and take up his cross, and follow Me."** We must deny 'self', humble self, crucify selfishness and self-centeredness, and submit to Jesus' instructions, i.e., keep YHVH's law and the Prophets and worship YHVH alone.

True repentance washes away our sin, we are forgiven, pardoned, justified, and made white as snow. And the reason YHVH is willing to do that is because of His mercy and grace shown to those who love Him enough to commit make Him their supreme authority. And God loves those who love Him and submit to His Divine authority – and that's what true repentance does. We may not keep them perfectly, but we will again repent when we fail.

And again, it's not the mechanical obedience that saves a person, nor do we merit God's saving grace, but by a willingness to obeying God honors Him, glorifies Him and that is an act of worship. We display a love for God and fearful respect of God by submitting to His Divine authority, and that is the type of character that God wants in His eternal Kingdom. And, that's in sharp contrast to those who dishonor God by rejecting His Divine authority by setting aside His laws and commands.

"**Salvation is by God's grace alone through faith alone**" and that's not just a New Testament concept, it comes from the Old Testament, it is embedded within the Ten Commandments written with the finger of God; Exodus 20:6, "**but showing mercy** (that's grace) **to thousands of generations** (that's forever), **to those who love Me and keep My commandments** (that's true faith)."

The law is a test of our love and loyalty to YHVH God. "**If you love Me you will keep my commandments**" (John 14:15). And to those whom YHVH God loves He will invite them into His kingdom to dine with Him (John 14:23).

All people have sinned and therefore all people need repentance. It's only by God's mercy that He allows us to repent, to be forgiven, to receive pardoned, be made white as snow, justified and have our sins blotted out.

Repentance results in the fruit of repentance, is that we stop sinning by keeping God's commandments, i.e., righteousness. And that happens when we have committed or recommitted ourselves to submit to YHVH God as our supreme authority, and if we do that we will obey all that He commanded. And that involves humbling and 'crucifying' self and installing YHVH on the throne of our hearts and minds, so that we do His will.

Jesus give us the key to repentance in Luke 9:23 (NKJV), **"Then He said to them all, "If anyone desires to come after Me, let him deny himself, and take up his cross daily, and follow Me."** Luke adds the word 'daily' letting us know that this is a lifetime struggle. Jesus said crucify your own 'self' or humble self, that is our self-will, self-love and selfishness.

The serpent beast told Eve that we can be our own supreme authority (god) and know good and evil for ourselves. Jesus said that's not how it will be if you want to enter God's eternal kingdom. Jesus told us to submit to his will, and his will was that we obey all that the Father said. He told us to worship YHVH alone (Matthew 4:10) and to keep YHVH's law and the Prophets (Matthew 5:17-18) - that is Jesus' will and that is the will of YHVH God.

Jesus told us to keep YHVH's 'law and the Prophets', but the Christian Church, using Paul's epistles, which tell everyone that they don't need to keep YHVH's laws, for Paul tells us that God's laws were 'nail to the cross', and Paul gives us 36 other reasons why we don't need to keep God's laws. When Christians accept Paul's lawless teachings and ignore Jesus' commands to keep YHVH's 'law and the Prophets', and they become lawless presumptuous sinners, violating God's law at will and never repenting. When we dismiss YHVH's laws, we end up deciding for ourselves what is 'good and evil', we thus become our own gods determining 'good and evil' for ourselves. At that point repentance is exactly what a sinner needs – repentance requires that we submit to YHVH's Divine authority and obey Jesus' commands.

## NO NEW COVENANT

Christianity teaches that it is under the New Covenant, and so Christians can ignore those Old Covenant laws and they just need to 'believe in Jesus'. We were taught that Jesus initiated the New Covenant with his blood that he shed for the forgiveness of our sins. And since he took the punishment for our sin, our sinning (violation of the Old Testament laws) is not a real big deal, because as long as we trust in Jesus our sins are forgiven and forgotten.

Contrary to popular belief, the Christian Church is not under the 'New Covenant'. You are probably saying, yes, we are under the New Covenant, because Jesus instituted the New Covenant at the Last Supper. Didn't he? No, he didn't, but, let's take a look at what Jesus really said;

Matthew 26:28 (NKJV), **"For this is My blood of the [a]new covenant, which is shed for many for the [b]remission of sins."**
Footnotes
a. Matthew 26:28 NU omits *new*
b. Matthew 26:28 *forgiveness*

The first footnote (a.) tells us that the most reliable Greek manuscripts did not originally have the word 'New' before the word 'covenant'. If Jesus wasn't referring to the 'New Covenant' in this verse, he was referring to what we call the 'Old Covenant'. The word 'new' was added by some scribe or copyist to some of the Greek texts to help us "understand" (or misunderstand) the text. So, re-writing that verse using the information from the footnotes, it reads;

What Jesus said was; Matthew 26:28, **"For this is My blood of the covenant, which is shed for many for the forgiveness of sins."**

To be redeemed, we must be in a covenant relationship with YHVH God. There are two covenants in the Scripture that we may fit under, the Old and the New.

Most people are familiar with the 'Old Covenant', and they believe that those under that Covenant (the Jews) are expected to keep the Law of Moses to be one of God's people and gain entrance into the Kingdom of God. And the wrongly believe that Christians are under the New Covenant, and they are saved by God's grace just for believing in Jesus.

People wrongly believe that those under the Old Covenant have to keep the laws of Moses to be right with God and saved. However they are completely wrong, for people under the Old Covenant were only saved by the grace of God – and it was not by keeping the law. The only way anyone was ever saved is by the grace of God.

In the Old Testament, i.e., the Old Covenant, salvation is by "God's grace alone through faith alone", and that was embedded in the Ten Commandments, written by the finger of God. Exodus 20:6, **"but showing mercy** *(grace, or lovingkindness)* **to thousands of generations** *(that's forever)*, **to those who love Me and keep My commandments** *(that's true faith)"*. **God loves those who love Him and keeps His commandments** – *that is Old Covenant.* And repentance is available for those who fail at keeping His commandments.

And yes, they were given the law to keep, just as Adam and Eve were given a law to test them. The results of the test will determine whether or not YHVH is their true God. We too have a law to keep, all of Jesus' commands, which tell us to keep YHVH's law and the Prophets, and to worship YHVH alone. The question then is, as it is today, will you submit to YHVH God's divine authority, or will you follow the dictates of your own heart.

And no, Jesus did not initiate the New Covenant, I know that we read what Jesus said during the Passover meal, Matthew 26:28, **"For this is My blood of the new covenant, which is shed for many for the remission of sins"**. However, if we look at the footnotes for that verse and the original Greek text, we will notice that the word **'new'** in not there, it was added by a translator. So Jesus is not referring to the New Covenant in that verse. Christians are not under the New Covenant, and most are not under the Old Covenant either.

Three Angels' Messages for the Christian Church

At the Passover event is when YHVH God, the God of Abraham, Isaac and Jacob, rescued ancient Israel from the Egyptians and brought them to the Promised Land – the were saved, or redeemed. And the message for us that if trust and obey that same God, He will deliver us into the Promised Land, through redemption.

When we read the New Covenant it is clear that the Christians are not in this covenant relationship with YHVH, it reads; **"But this is the covenant that I will make with the house of Israel after those days, says YHVH: I will put My law** *(Torah)* **in their minds, and write it on their hearts; and I will be their God, and they shall be My people. 34 No more shall every man teach his neighbor, and every man his brother, saying, 'Know YHVH,' for they all shall know Me, from the least of them to the greatest of them, says YHVH. For I will forgive their iniquity, and their sin I will remember no more"** (Jeremiah 31:33-34). Is this the Covenant that God has with Christians? No, it can't be, none of it fits. As a condition of the Covenant YHVH said, **"I will be their God"**. However, YHVH is not the God of Christianity, they have rejected as their God and instead they worship the Trinity. If YHVH was their God they'd obey all He said and worship Him alone, but they don't do that. The god of Christianity is the Trinity, and they predominately focus on Jesus. And YHVH God is not part of the Trinity, He will not accept the position or role for He said He alone is God and He is a jealous God and will not share His glory or worship with another god. So, any Christians who will not accept YHVH as their one true God, cannot be not part of the New Covenant.

In addition, the Christian Church will not keep God's Torah law, which God said He in the New Covenant that He would write in our minds and on our hearts, so that we will remember His law and have the desire to do it. But the Christian Church rejects God's Torah law, claiming that it is passed away or nailed to the cross. They violate it at will, and feel no guilt or shame because they don't feel that they are under the jurisdiction of YHVH's Torah law. And if they did feel bad about what they did they would go to YHVH God to be forgiven they'd go to Jesus. So those in the Christian Church are certainly not a participants in the New Covenant.

Within the New Covenant, Jeremiah 31:34, YHVH said **'for they all shall know me from the least to the greatest**." That certainly hasn't happened yet. But we will see that in the Messianic age; Isaiah 11:9, **"They shall not hurt nor destroy in all My holy mountain, For the earth shall be full of the knowledge of YHVH As the waters cover the sea."**

And the Christian Church is certainly not under the Old Covenant either. The Commandments of God were the stipulations of the Old Covenant. The First Commandment requires participants in the Old Covenant to worship YHVH alone; Exodus 20:2-3, **"I am YHVH your God, who brought you out of the land of Egypt, out of the house of bondage, you shall have no other**

**gods before Me."** Christians reject that commandment to worship the Trinity instead – because their church tells them to. And they violate the Second Commandment by worshiping a man as God – because their church tells them to. And most Christians reject the Forth Commandment to keep YHVH's Sabbath day holy, and they go to church on Sundays – because their church tells them to. And since Christians don't keep the Commandments of God, which are the stipulations of the Old Covenant, they are not under the Old Covenant or the New Covenant. Isaiah 24:5, **"The earth is also defiled under its inhabitants, Because they have transgressed the laws, Changed the ordinance, Broken the everlasting covenant."**

But, what about Jesus words, "the blood of the Covenant", in Matthew 26:28? The Old Covenant was sealed with blood. Exodus 20:6-7, **"And Moses took half the blood and put it in basins, and half the blood he sprinkled on the altar. 7 Then he took the Book of the Covenant and read in the hearing of the people. And they said, "All that YHVH has said we will do, and be obedient." 8 And Moses took the blood, sprinkled it on the people, and said, "This is the blood of the covenant which YHVH has made with you according to all these words."** So the blood of a bull was the blood of the covenant, and it was not the shed blood of a sin sacrifice. The covenant blood was to seal the words of the covenant. In other words, Israel was as a participant in that covenant so long as they obeyed YHVH's words – the words of the covenant. That is, God would accept them as His so long as they obeyed His laws.

So, Jesus used the grape juice to represent his blood, and all who drank of it are sealed into the covenant. Those who partake in the grape juice are participants in the covenant, so long as they obey Jesus' words. When they fail to keep Jesus' words, to keep YHVH's 'law and the Prophets' (Matthew 5:17-18) and to worship YHVH alone (Matthew 4:10), they have broken covenant.

In John 6:53-63 we learn that Jesus' flesh and blood are metaphors for his words. And he has the words of eternal life. Jesus then told us that we can participate in a covenant relationship with God by abiding in his words of eternal life; and that includes keeping YHVH's law and the Prophets, and worship YHVH God as the one true God – as Jesus commanded (Matthew 4:10, 5:17-19, Mark 12:29, Luke 4:8, John 17:3).

So, the stipulations of either of the Covenants requires that we accept YHVH alone as our God and we obey His voice (spoken by Him or Jesus). Here, Christians fail at keeping the stipulations of the New and the Old Covenant, because YHVH is not their one true God.

Christians need to reject the doctrine of the Trinity, and embrace YHVH as our one true God and submit to His Divine authority a expressed in the 'law and the Prophets'.

## IS JESUS GOD?

The Scriptures never call Jesus God, and Jesus never claimed to be God. Jesus always referred to God as someone other than himself (John 14:1, 17:3). Jesus prayed to YHVH God (Matthew 6, John 17) and worshiped YHVH God (John 4:22-23), whom he said was his 'God and Father' (John 20:17).

People claim the Jesus was God because he was worshiped and accepted that worship. However, what they fail to tell you is that the same Greek word that is translated as 'worship' can also be translated as 'bow down' or somehow showing reverence. And many translations don't use the word 'worship' but rather they say, 'bowed down', as in showing reverence. And it's not surprising the people would show great reverence to someone they considered to be a great prophet (Luke 7:17), miracle worker (Acts 2:22), speaking YHVH's words with YHVH's authority (John 14:10), and great teacher or rabbi (Matthew 22:6). We'd show great reverence to such a person ourselves.

Jesus actually denied he was God time and in many ways, such as John 4:22-23 where it said he was among the Jews who worshiped God, and John 20:17 where he said that he had a God and a Father and He was the same God and Father his disciples had (John 20:17). Or when Jesus said he was not good, but God alone was good. (Matthew 19:17) and the many other times he defined God as some other than himself.

Jesus himself told us to worship YHVH alone (Matthew 4:10), and YHVH told us to worship Himself alone (Exodus 20:2-3) so to worship Jesus or a Trinity would be to dishonor both Jesus and YHVH by rejecting their direct commands. And such a person is an idolater and will not be allowed into God's kingdom.

YHVH God commanded that He be worshiped alone. And we must do that because YHVH God is a jealous God who will not share His glory, praise or worship with another god, and He is a consuming fire for those who worship anyone other that Himself.

So clearly Jesus is not the God, but he refers to himself as 'a god'. Many people in the Old Testament were referred to as 'god'. The title 'god' was often used with people who received and spoke God's word. John 10:34-35, **"Jesus answered them, "Is it not written in your law, 'I said, "You are gods"'? 35 If He called them gods, to whom the word of God came (and the Scripture cannot be broken)".** Jesus quoting Psalm 82:6, and Isaiah 41:23, was referring to himself as a god **"to whom the word of God came"**. And that clarified John 1:1 where it read, **"In the beginning was the word, the word**

**was with the God** *(YHVH)* **and the word was a god** (Jesus)". Jesus, by his own admission, was not God, but a god (i.e., prophet).

End of Chapter

## CHAPTER 2 – REVELATION'S SEVEN CHURCHES

## REVELATION CHAPTER 2-3 - LETTERS TO THE SEVEN CHURCHES

What is it Jesus wants us to hear and understand in his letters to the Seven Churches? Jesus is showing us how the Church has strayed from the Word of God. The Churches have over time abandoned God's word and have adopted corrupt practices, compromised their faith, turned from God's way and have gone their own way. And it's only when we understand how bad the church has gotten that we will understand the need for the three angels' messages. If the Church was right with God, God would be encouraging them to continue as they are, praising and blessing them, and they wouldn't need the correction, the rebukes, the calls to repentance and the Everlasting Gospel. And God wouldn't be calling them to leave Babylon the Great.

The Church has fallen from God's grace, and thus God will call His people out and inflict them with the plagues. The purposes of the future plagues are two-fold; the plagues are to get the people to repent, and to punish those who will not repent.

Without dealing with who, where or when each of the Seven Churches are in time and history, we can learn from God's messages to each of them. God's messages for morality, righteousness, His warnings, rebukes, corrections and instructions for godly living are timeless, so what He said to each of the churches applies to us today.

God's letter to each of the churches provides warnings of judgment, but not without corrective instruction, and there are calls to be righteous for each Church. But these instructions, rebukes, corrections and warnings are also meant for all those who hear and read the letters. In the same way Isaiah, Jeremiah, Hosea, Amos and the rest of the prophets warned the people about committing idolatry, social injustices, and cruelty, those warnings were also meant for us, since YHVH God's words are timeless truths, because He does not change. If Isaiah's and Jeremiah's messages were only pertinent for their times, their writings would have long been discarded.

In Matthew 5:17-20, Jesus told us to obey YHVH's **'Law and Prophets' until heaven and earth pass away.** We must heed the prophets' warnings, and heed the letters to the churches, to avoid making the same mistakes that we now know will bring about God's judgment.

As we read about the Seven Churches we have to remember that they were all founded by Paul, the false apostle. Since they were all founded by Paul they all had seeds of corruptions planted in them. Tare seeds planted along with the good seeds (Matthew 13:24-30). What is the problem with Paul's teachings? He was lawless and that will be explained in the last chapter of this book.

As I pointed out, the warnings to each of the Seven Churches, you will see consistent themes; 1. Keep God's law, 2. Don't be deceived or led astray from keeping God's law, 3. Repent when you fail, 4. Be faithful for the time is short.

## THE MESSAGES TO THE SEVEN CHURCHES:

**Ephesus** (Revelation 2:1-7) – "**I know your deeds**". What were their deeds? God's Law, the Torah, requires that we all do deeds of love, mercy, and compassion. God said, 'nothing is hidden from Me, I know what you are doing'. God commends them in Revelation 2:2b, "**And you have tested those who say they are apostles and are not, and have found them liars**". There were those that came to them claiming to be Apostles, but they discerned that they were liars (Pail?). How did they determine that? They must have read their Scriptures. The Scriptures give several tests to determine if someone is valid Apostle or not. First, an "Apostle" was only an Apostle if they had witnessed the life and death and resurrection of Jesus. (Acts 1:21-22) Second, Jesus said that we can know them by their fruit (Matthew 7:15-20), and third, Isaiah said if they don't teach according to the law and the Prophets, there's no light in them (Isaiah 8:20). Those who possess apostleship would have to be faithful believers, passing Isaiah's test and Jesus' test before they could even be considered as an 'Apostle'. One way or another, there were those that claimed to be Apostles but failed the test. God commends the Ephesians for that level of discernment. That was very admirable of them. We should do the same with our religious leaders, examine their fruit, are they keeping God's laws? And do they teach and preach according to the 'law and the Prophets'? If not, there is no light in them.

Lamentations 2:14, "**Your prophets have seen for you false and deceptive visions; They have not uncovered your iniquity, To bring back your captives, But have envisioned for you false prophecies and delusions.**" In the time of Jeremiah, the religious leaders were teaching people falsely and did '**not uncover the people's sins**'. So commentators say that in the Hebrew it is says that they 'whitewashed' peoples sins. Either way, the religious leaders were indifferent to the law of God and how people violated it, we could say that they were the lawless leaders and teaching people to be lawless. Paul and the Pharisee were convinced that they were God's chosen, the 'elect of God's grace' and so they were automatically saved and so keeping the 'law and the Prophets' was not important. And that's exactly what Paul wrote in his epistles and taught his churches.

What has changed today? The religious leaders (Jeremiah 6:14) says, **'peace, peace'**, that is everything is fine, don't worry **'you will surely not die'** – while the people were lawless and condemned – the people in our churches are lawless, and they are told that's OK because they are saved by grace, saved by the blood, saved by a sinner's prayer, saved by church sacraments, saved by religion... nothing has changed.

The Ephesians were also commended for having separated themselves from the wicked. But they were also admonished for having forsaken God and God's law that they once kept, **"Remember therefore from where you have fallen"**. They have fallen from their first love, and Jesus told us what that first love was; Mark 12:29-30, **"The most important one," answered Jesus, "is this: 'Hear, O Israel: YHVH our God, YHVH is one. 30 Love YHVH your God with all your heart and with all your soul and with all your mind and with all your strength**." The churches have turned Jesus into a God, and placed their affections on him and ignore YHVH whom is supposed to be their first love. YHVH God is to be our first love – and if you love God you will keep His commandments (Exodus 20:6, John 14:15 and 1John 5:2) and the First Commandment (Exodus 20:2-3) tells us to worship 'YHVH' alone. When we accept other gods, even Jesus or the Trinity, we no longer place the same value on YHVH's Commandments. We keep the laws of whoever, or whatever is our god. If we don't keep YHVH's commandments, it's because He is not our 'real' god – and we have some other lawless supreme authority. That lawless authority is the one that told us we don't have to keep YHVH's laws – and we accepted its authority over God's Divine authority.

It seems as though the Ephesians started off good, but gradually had 'fallen' as they were persuaded by certain people to forsake God's laws and exalt Jesus as God. When we worship Jesus instead of YHVH, we focus on forgiveness and grace and forget YHVH's commandments, figuring that all the law is nailed to the cross anyway – perhaps that was their error. They were falling away from keeping God's commandments, that was the evidence that they had fallen from their first love, and therefore they were called on to repent. According to 1John 3:4, sin is transgression of God's law. To repent of your sin is then to stop transgressing God's law and start keeping God's law. Jesus told us to be faithful, though you may be persecuted and even put to death, but you will receive a crown of life. In other words, our obedience to YHVH is more important than our own life – and if He is our first love, that's not a problem.

Those who repent of their sins, i.e., overcome their sinfulness, and will eat from the Tree of Life in the Paradise of God. In other words, they will receive eternal life and live in the Kingdom of their God if they keep God's commandments. The Paradise of God points back to the Garden of Eden.

To their credit they hated the deeds of the Nicolaitans which God also hates. Little is known about the Nicolaitans, but the Greek word means 'to conquer the people' or 'victory over the people'. Many believe this was ecclesiastical hierarchy, such as we see in the churches today; where they have: popes, conference president, cardinals, bishops, pastors, deacons, elders and they all have authority over the laity. And the laity then relies on those 'religious authorities' above them for religious direction and religious truth – and that type of system inherently leaves the laity vulnerable for other to tell them Biblical truths. And that led to abuses, lies, traditions, and lawlessness all being taught as Biblical truth. And that ecclesiastical hierarchy (i.e., the Nicolaitans) is in contrast to the self-autonomous, self-ruled and governed synagogues. In the synagogues they only hierarchy was the word of God.

The Nicolaitans ended up being antinomian, that is they were lawless, and had rejected God's law. Perhaps they were like today's church, saying that it wasn't necessary to keep the law of God, because Jesus died on the cross.

The problem with this hierarchical structure is that one bad pope, cardinal or bishop will negatively affect all those under him, this is a recipe for corruption. For instance, if the Pope invents a new doctrine, the entire church must comply to accept it. This also creates a dependency for the people, where they will rely on those people in ecclesiastical positions above them instead of seeking to study and know God's will for themselves. That hierarchy would tend to create a trust, dependency and reliance on the Church leadership, rather than on God.

Today the entire Christian Church promotes that their people be dependent on their church, and their pastor or priest and all who above them. They are considered to be bad Christians if they don't attend the church services weekly or at least often. (This was much prevalent prior to this century). That mindset is the result of the thinking of the Nicolatians – follow the instruction and teaching of the leaders.

In the Jewish culture, the center for a family's religious and spiritual activity is the home. People studied at home, prayed at home and celebrated their Jewish holy days at home. Nicolatians want to destroy that concept and insist attendance at their weekly service, where we can be spoon feed church doctrine by the pastor or priest, taking over the role as the family's spiritual leader. The result of these Church Doctrines, is that the people are worshiping Jesus and the Trinity and rejecting of God's 'law and the Prophets'.

Jesus then said be faithful unto death, though you may be persecuted and even put to death, but if that happens you will receive a crown of life. If they repent of their sins, or overcome them, they will eat from the Tree of Life in the Paradise of God. If we repent of our sins, i.e., overcome them, we too will eat from the Tree of Life in the Paradise of God.

Jesus was calling on them to acknowledge their sins and repent. Why weren't they doing that? They were founded and taught by Paul. Paul gives us 36 reasons why we don't need to keep God's law. In Acts 21:20-21 he was rebuked for teaching that it wasn't necessary to keep God's laws.

To each church there is a final warning is given to listen to the 'spirit' ('breath' carrying God's word, or word of God) written to the seven churches.

Jesus said, "**He who has an ear, let him hear what the Spirit says to the churches**." If you have ears (as all people do), listen to and heed these words they are meant for all people with ears! He wasn't just speaking to the church in Ephesus, he was speaking to you and me – and all people with ears.

**Smyrna** (Revelation 2:8-11) – The church was undergoing persecution so the message Jesus gave them was a message that is applicable to us when we undergo persecution for the sake of the Gospel, as Jesus told us in Matthew 5:10, "**Blessed are those who are persecuted for righteousness' sake, For theirs is the kingdom of heaven.**" He also tells us that religious persecution will come from those within the church by professed believers. Churches have manmade doctrines and creeds. When someone doesn't accept or practice according to those 'false' doctrines and creeds, they are called heretics. Throughout the centuries, churches persecuted 'heretics'. A lawless church will persecute people who keep God's law. A church that practices idolatry by worshiping the Trinity will persecute those who worship YHVH God alone. It seems that lawless people are angered when they see true believes keeping God's law – and thus they persecute them to get them to stop. But Jesus said be faithful until death, and you will be rewarded with a crown of life.

Jesus also said, "**I know the blasphemy of those who say they are Jews and are not, but are a synagogue of Satan.**" Who were these "Jews"? They were the 'believers' or 'Jewish believers' at the writing of the Book, there was no such thing as a 'Christian' or 'Christian Church'. The early believers in the Scriptures were all 'Jews' who believed Jesus to be the Messiah and they kept the 'law and the prophets' and worshiped YHVH God as Jesus commanded, Acts 24:14 "**However, I admit that I worship the God of our ancestors as a follower of the Way, which they call a sect. I believe everything that is in accordance with the Law** *(Torah)* **and that is written in the Prophets**", and that's just what Jesus told us to do (Matthew 4:10 and 5:17-20) keep the 'law and the prophets'.

Apparently there were some among them who were blaspheming God – most likely Paul's pagan converts, who never really converted. They adopted the name 'Jew', allowed themselves to be baptized, believe Jesus died and was resurrected and they then considered themselves to saved believers – but they were taught that they didn't need to keep God's law, and so they rejected it.

To blaspheme God is to say wrong or evil about Him and malign His character. To teach that God doesn't care if we are lawless is to pervert justice, and that maligns God's Character. To say that God is a Trinity, after He has told us so many times that He is the only true God, is to blaspheme God, because it is distorting God's character, demoting His Divine authority by saying that there are two other gods equal to Him. It would also be a blasphemy to tell people that they don't need to keep God's laws, telling them that they can spurn God's Divine authority, ignoring or setting aside His laws, and commands, is treating Him to be less than God, and thus dishonoring Him and blaspheming Him.

## THE SYNAGOGUE OF SATAN

There is very little said about the '**Synagogue of Satan**' in the Book of the Revelation, only 2 references; Revelation 2:9 and 3:9. But from those two references, and from their context, we can gleam some details about the **Synagogue of Satan.** What is the '**Synagogue of Satan**'? First, we must understand that the word 'synagogue' means a common meeting place where the Jews, and the early believers, who were also Jews, came together on Sabbath for communal worship and study together. At the time of the writing of the Book of the Revelation there was no such thing as a 'church' buildings, the word 'church' describes a group of "called out people", the true believers. The 'church' people met in a synagogue. So the Scriptures uses the phrase '**synagogue of Satan**' instead of '**church of Satan**' because would grammatically makes no sense since a 'church' was not a place or a building. The phrase '**synagogue of Satan**' was never intended to denigrate the Jews or speak negatively about them. As far as the Scriptures go, the 'Jews' who follow Jesus' teachings are the only true believers and true worshipers of YHVH God, and those who are true Jewish believers are YHVH God's chosen people meeting on the weekly Sabbath in synagogues.

So the '**Synagogue of Satan**' would be a group of people who claimed to be Jewish believers in Jesus as the Messiah, but followed the lawless teachings, or doctrines of Satan. What were the teachings of Satan? Satan's principle teaching, as we saw in the Garden of Eden, is rebellion against God's authority, that is 'lawlessness', that is, teaching people that they don't have to keep the law(s) of God. In rejecting the law(s) of God, a person becomes a lawless presumptuous sinner who sees nothing wrong in breaking some, or all, of God's law(s) and therefore they feel no remorse for their sins and will not repent. By rejecting any of God's laws, they are rejecting God's Divine authority over them, which puts them in a state of rebellion against God, and makes them an enemy of God (James 4:4).

In the Book of Genesis, following Satan's deception, Eve became 'lawless' when she was deceived by Satan (serpent beast) to set God's command aside to obey the serpent, and in doing that she dismiss God's authority – and did not remorse over her wrong doing, nor would she repent when she was confronted. When we are lawless, rejecting God's law(s), we dishonor Jesus who told us to keep the law of God, and we dishonor God, by rejecting His Divine authority which is expressed in His law(s), His direct commands. The lawless will have no place in God's kingdom (Matthew 7, Matthew 13). Those in the Synagogue of Satan were those who practiced lawlessness.

Revelation 2:9-10, (NKJV) **"I know your works, tribulation, and poverty (but you are rich); and *I know* the blasphemy of those who say they are Jews and are not, but *are* a synagogue of Satan.**
**Do not fear any of those things which you are about to suffer. Indeed, the devil is about to throw *some* of you into prison, that you may be tested, and you will have tribulation ten days. Be faithful until death, and I will give you the crown of life."**

In these two verses we see a contrast between two types of believers. While all the true believers were 'Jews' or converts to Judaism. So there were Jews who kept God's laws, and there were the Gentile Jews, who were lawless disciples of Paul (Acts 21:20-21). We see in these verses that there are the true Jews and the false Jews (Gentiles). The false Jews called themselves Jews, but they are Jews in name only. Who is a true Jew? Luke 3:8 (NKJV), **"Therefore bear fruits worthy of repentance, and do not begin to say to yourselves, 'We have Abraham as *our* father.' For I say to you that God is able to raise up children to Abraham from these stones."** There were many Jews, **'children of Abraham'**, many, or most were physical descendent of Abraham. But being a physical **'Child of Abraham'**, means nothing to God, what God wants is for a person to bear the **"fruits worthy of repentance'**. What's the **'fruit of repentance'**? Repentance literally means to 'turn around'. So to repent of your sin, means to turn away from your sin and go the other way. Or, we could say, stop breaking God's law (sin) and start keeping it. Or, we could just say, 'Keep God's law'.

The **'fruit of repentance'** is what repentance produces, keeping God's law, God calls it righteousness. Luke 5:32 (NKJV), **"I have not come to call *the* righteous, but sinners, to repentance."** Jesus came to call the sinners (law breakers) to repentance (law keeping) so they may be righteous before God by keeping God's law. Righteousness is keeping God's laws, Luke 1:6 (NKJV), **"And they were both righteous before God, walking in all the commandments and ordinances of the Lord blameless."** To follow Jesus' teachings by the keeping the **'Law and the Prophets'** (Matthew 5:17-20) as Jesus commanded, would make a person righteous. And by keeping the **'law**

**and the Prophets'**, as Jesus commanded, we become what he and his disciples were, effectively you become a Biblical Jew.  Being righteous by God's standards does not mean that a person never sins, it means that they truly repent when they do sin.

True Biblical Jews are those who live according to the Scriptures, keeping God's commandments and ordinances and follow Jesus' teachings (the faith of Jesus) and repenting when they fail.  Those who say they are Jews (believers) and are not, are the lawless Jews (mostly former Gentiles) who do not keep the commandments of God or His ordinances, nor do they keep the 'faith of Jesus', therefore they do not remorse when they sin or repent when they fail. They are 'lawless', no doubt following Paul's teachings to set God's law(s) aside, some of God's laws, or all of them, which makes them presumptuous sinners.

Since Paul was the founder of these seven churches, the lawless issues they are having is not surprising.  Today's churches that follow Paul's teachings, to exclusion of Jesus' teachings, are having the same lawless issues. In Acts 21:20-21 Paul is confronted with the Jews in Jerusalem and told how many of their converts are zealous for the law. Yet, they are told that Paul has told his converts to ignore or reject the law of God.  And that lawless condition is reflected in the letters to the seven churches.

If we even to set just one of God's laws aside, and reject it, it is saying, 'no', to God and rejecting His Divine authority over us – and it's also to reject Jesus' word, because he told us to keep God's commandments.  Jesus said, Matthew 5:17-19, (NKJV) **"Do not think that I came to destroy the Law or the Prophets. I did not come to destroy but to fulfill. 18 For assuredly, I say to you, till heaven and earth pass away, one jot or one tittle will by no means pass from the law till all is fulfilled. 19 Whoever therefore breaks one of the least of these commandments, and teaches men so, shall be called least in the kingdom of heaven; but whoever does and teaches** *them,* **he shall be called great in the kingdom of heaven."** John 8:51, (NKJV) "**Most assuredly, I say to you, if anyone keeps My word he shall never see death."**  So, those who will keep YHVH's '**law and the prophets'** will never '**see death**'.  Those who refuse to keep the '**law and the Prophets'** and say, 'I'm not under those commandments, they are not for me', will **'see death'.**

Many people are told that they are '**not under the law but under grace'** so they don't have to keep God's laws, so they eat their Easter Sunday Ham dinners and sin like the devil.  They figure that they can be in rebellion against God, reject this commandments, despise His Word, snub His Divine authority, 'hate' Him, sin freely, live like the devil, and God will still love them and give them saving grace on Judgment day. But the truth is, God wouldn't want those people in the Kingdom of Heaven.  God only gives saving grace to those whom He loves. And the Scriptures tell us how to get God to love us with that kind of love. The Scriptures tell us that God loves those who love Him and keep His commandments (Exodus 20:6 and John 14:21, 22-23).

In Revelation 2:9 we read, **"The blasphemy of those who say they are Jews and are not, but *are* a <u>synagogue of Satan</u>"**. "Jew" was the common term for believers. The true believers were all Jews, they kept YHVH's law and the Prophets, they believed Jesus to be the Messiah and they worshipped YHVH God (the Father) who was the God of the Jews. For someone to say that they are Jews (Christians), while they are not, means that they were Jews (Christian) by name only, not Jewish in practice, that is, they did not keep YHVH's 'law and the Prophets' or they didn't not worship YHVH alone – which makes one a Biblical Jew (true Christian). The false Jews blaspheme by the worship of someone other than YHVH and (or) their rejection of YHVH 'law and the Prophets'. Thus they belong to the **'synagogue of Satan'**. To call yourself a 'Jew' or a 'Christian' and then live like the devil is to blaspheme God by giving Him a bad name.

Is a true Christian one who keeps all the creeds and doctrines of the Christian Church, or is a true Christian one that follows all the teachings of Christ? I would say the latter, but the Church would say the former.

As we read in the Book of the Revelation, Satan is the 'serpent beast' and it is his lawless teachings given to us by the Christian Church (I.e., the beast and his image), that is the source of the **Mark of the Beast**. Satan is the serpent beast who lies and deceives with his poisonous venom, which is his 'lawless' teaching deceived Eve. Just as with Eve in Book of Genesis, Satan's deadliest deceit causes people to practice 'lawlessness' rejecting YHVH God's Divine authority, so those in the **'synagogue of Satan'** teaching and practicing **'lawlessness'** while claiming to be God's people (Christians). Being 'lawless' while claiming to be one of God chosen people gives God a negative image, tarnishes His character, makes religion stink in the eyes of those watching, and it misrepresents God to the nations, and thus they blaspheme God by the rejection His Divine authority over them. That is how the lawless (false Jews and false believers) were blaspheming God.

Notice that Jesus tells those who are not part of the **'synagogue of Satan'** to endure, while being tested, and if faithful unto death and they will receive a **'crown of life'**. How do they receive a **'crown of life'**? By enduring and being "**faithful until death**". Being 'Faithful' to what? 'What happens if they are not faithful? We'll see.

The saints of God are called to faithfully '**endur**e', or 'persevere'? James tells us more about perseverance or endurance to receive the 'crown of life'. James 1:12 (NKJV), **"Blessed *is* the man who endures temptation; for when he has been approved, he will receive the crown of life which the Lord has** promised to those who love Him." James tells us that if we '**endure temptation**' we will receive a '**crown of life**'. What is it to '**endure temptation**'? It means to avoid the sin that temptation leads to. Another way to say that is to keep the law even when you are tempted to break it. And that is perfectly compatible with what Jesus said in Revelation 14:12 (ESV), **"Here is the endurance of the saints; here are those who keep the commandments of God and the faith of Jesus."** To reject temptation and the enticing benefits that go along with it, to do God's will, it is to sacrifice our self-will, self-desire, self-love, and selfishness, and that is a more pleasing sacrifice to YHVH God than sheep, goat, rams and oxen.

In contrast to those in the '**synagogue of Satan**', are the true Jews are to be faithful unto death, or the patiently endure to **"keep the commandments of God and the faith of Jesus."**

**Revelation 2:12-17**, church in Pergamos. In Revelation 2:14 we read, **"But I have a few things against you, because you have there those who hold the doctrine of Balaam, who taught Balak to put a stumbling block before the children of Israel, to eat things sacrificed to idols, and to commit sexual immorality."**

In Numbers 25:1-16 we read about an incident that happened to Israel; **"Now Israel remained in Acacia Grove, and the people began to commit harlotry with the women of Moab. 2 They invited the people to the sacrifices of their gods, and the people ate and bowed down to their gods. 3 So Israel was joined to Baal of Peor, and the anger of YHVH was aroused against Israel."** The men of Israel had sexual relations with the Midianite women and in exchange the men offered sacrifices to the Midianite's god, Baal of Peor. The sexual sin was bad, but it is forgivable, for when YHVH is our God we can go to Him for forgiveness, so long as we truly repent. However, the Midianite women enticed the Israelite men to worship their gods and when YHVH is not our sole God, we cannot receive forgiveness from Him. That false worship is the reason that the men were executed. We read in Deuteronomy 4:3-4, **"Your eyes have seen what YHVH did at Baal Peor; for YHVH your God has destroyed from among you all the men who followed Baal of Peor. 4 But you who held fast to YHVH your God are alive today, every one of you."** YHVH God issued a death decree against anyone who the not 'hold fast to YHVH as their God', but instead worshiped other gods, Baal of Peor. YHVH was, and still is, a Jealous God, and a burning fire – that means that idolatry will be judged by death. We see this problem again in the book of the Revelation where 'harlotry and idol worship' appear together and we see that those in the Church have fallen for the 'teachings of Balaam'. Balaam's plan was for the men to fornicate with the 'women' and thus be defiled themselves with the worship of false gods. The 'women' in the Book of the Revelation are the Great Harlot (the Roman Catholic Church) and her many harlot daughters (the Protestant Churches). And Revelation 14:4-5 tells us that those who did not follow the teachings of the 'LAMB' were defied by the 'women' who enticed them to worship false gods (the Trinity). The 'Lamb' told us to worship YHVH alone (Matthew 4:10) and to keep YHVH's 'law and the Prophets'.

Idolatry, is the worship of anyone other the 'YHVH' God, i.e., violation of the First Commandment. YHVH God has not changed, He tells us that He alone is to be worshiped, and that is His First Commandment written in stone by the finger of God (Exodus 20:2-3).

Revelation 3:9-10 (NKJV), **"Indeed I will make *those* of the synagogue of Satan, who say they are Jews and are not, but lie—indeed I will make them come and worship before your feet, and to know that I have loved you. 10 Because you have kept My command to persevere, I also will keep you from the hour of trial which shall come upon the whole world, to test those who dwell on the earth."**

"**Worship**" can also mean to 'bow down', 'show reverence' or 'to serve', which would be a better translation here. Those from the '**synagogue of Satan**' don't actually worship the true believers as gods. The true believers would not allow that, for all 'worship' belongs to YHVH God. Jesus said, **"indeed I will make them come and worship before your feet" (vs. 9)**, it sounds like Jesus will use his rod of iron to make those false Jews serve, or submit to, the true Jewish believers.

Notice; in Revelation 3:10 it says of the true Jews that God promises to love them. Why would God love them but not love those in the **Synagogue of Satan**? Where is that promise in Scriptures? '**God loves those who love Him and keep His commandments**' (Exodus 20:6) and **"He who has My commandments and keeps them, it is he who loves Me. And he who loves Me will be loved by My Father, and I will love him and manifest Myself to him."** (John 14:21).

And since God loves the obedient Jews for keeping His commandments, God will spare them "**from the hour of trial which shall come upon the whole world, to test those who dwell on the earth.**" The true Biblical Jews who have kept the commandments of God and the faith of Jesus and therefore will have the 'seal of God'. Those in the '**synagogue of Satan**' have the 'Mark of the Beast' and will be subjected to fiery trials.

All people will fall into one of two categories, either the will have the '**Mark of the Beast**' or the '**Seal of God**'. Those in the '**synagogue of Satan**' are the lawless, who will receive the '**Mark of the Beast**' and will not receive a '**crown of life**'. Those who keep the commandments of God and the faith of Jesus will have the '**Seal of God**' and receive a '**crown of life**' (God's saving grace).

As I mentioned before, those who reject one or more of God's commandments, or laws, are in rebellion against God's Divine authority. They may not feel like they are in rebellion because they have been deceived, but they are by their not accepting God's authority over them. They may not feel like sinners, but they are sinners by breaking God's commandments (1John 3:4)– even if they don't think the law is for them. They may not feel like they hate God, but according to God's definition of 'hate' (Exodus 20:5), they hate God. They may feel that they love God, but the Bible says that we are to show our love for by keeping His commandments (1John 5:3) – so by God's definition, they don't love God. They may ever think that God loves them, but the Scriptures tell us that God loves those who love Him by keeping His commandments (Exodus 20:6, John 14:21, 23-24) and they don't keep God's commandments. They may even think that they are friends of God, but God views them as 'enemies of God' (James 4:4) whom God considers to 'hate' Him (Exodus 20:5). I'll bet your church never told you any of this.

At the expense of sounding redundant, I will repeat the main message of the Scripture, including the Book of the Revelation, because it is so very important, "**God loves those who love Him and keep His commandments**" and to them, He will give saving grace. And those who reject God's Divine authority by ignoring or setting aside His law and Commands are actually blaspheming God by spurning His Divine authority.

Jesus told them to repent, or overcome their sins, and then they will not be hurt by the second death, in other words they will receive eternal life.

Jesus said, "**He who has an ear, let him hear what the Spirit says to the churches**." If you have ears (as all people do), listen to these words they are meant for all people! He wasn't just speaking to the church in Smyrna, he was speaking to you and me.

<u>**Pergamum**</u> (Revelation 2:12-17) – Vs. 12 "**And you hold fast to My name, and did not deny My faith even in the days in which Antipas**". "**My Name**" has to do with character and testimony. When we hold fast to Jesus' name we are holding fast to his teaching. To reject his teachings would be to deny him. To '**not deny My faith**' is to be steadfastly faithful, even under persecutions to keep God's law and precepts – that was Jesus' faith, and Jesus was a law keeping, God fearing Jew. He tells us to be strong even though sin and Satan's minions are all around us, to harass and persecute us. Today the persecution is more in the form a peer-pressure, family-pressure, social-pressure and the lost of fellowship.

At the time of Pergamum, as today, some are falling at the false teachings which tell people that they don't need to keep God's law, and by setting aside God's law they are not holding fast to Jesus' name (his teachings) and they are denying his faith. Jesus' testimony includes his teachings, and

Jesus clearly and repeatedly told us to keep God's law and the Prophets and to worship YHVH alone, but these words are ignored by the entire Christian Church, thus people can enjoy the Easter Sunday Ham Dinner, and worship the Trinity on Sundays, without guilt or shame.

They were also eating unclean food and practicing sexual immorality, so they needed to repent and turn back to God's laws. Jesus rebuked them saying that they hold to the teaching of the Nicolaitans (lawless teaching) which He also hates. Then Jesus told them to repent. Jesus said if they don't repent, he himself will fight against them. Then he said that if they, repent, which is to overcome their sins, he will give them some of the hidden manna, a white stone and a new name (those are all promises of eternal life in the Kingdom of God). But they must listen, heed and obey what the 'spirit' (Word of God) says.

In Galatians 5:19-21, Paul list **'uncleanness'** as one of the sins that will keep people out of the Kingdom of God, and that would only be true if Paul was convinced that we need to keep the laws of God. We learn from the Old Testament that there are a few ways in which a person could contact uncleanness. One way is eating unclean meats. Yet the churches today practice such things as Easter Sunday Ham dinners. That is rejecting God's command to keep Passover, it is rejecting God's command to worship on Sabbath, and it is rejecting God's command to avoid pork. Those who do need to repent before it is too late.

Jesus said, "**He who has an ear, let him hear what the Spirit says to the churches**." If you have ears (as all people do), listen to these words which are meant for all people! He wasn't just speaking to the church in Pergamum, he was speaking to you and me.

**Thyatira** (Revelation 2:18-29) – A reminder that Jesus will judge us, and he knows all about us, specifically our deeds by which we will be judged. (Romans 2:5-6, "**But in accordance with your hardness and your impenitent heart you are treasuring up for yourself wrath in the day of wrath and revelation of the righteous judgment of God, 6 who "will render to each one according to his deeds")**. But in spite of their good deeds they were allowing errors to come into their midst, mainly lawlessness. Someone has convinced them that it's not important to keep all of God's laws, because they will be '**saved by grace**'. They were taught by a 'woman' (which is a religious system in the Book of Revelations) this one called Jezebel. Jezebel was a worshiper of false gods. What false God did these people worship? While the text doesn't tell us, an intelligent guess would be that they worshiped Jesus, and the Trinity. Jesus is not God, never claimed to be God, told us he was not God and he told us to worship YHVH, Our Father.

Those who follow Jezebel's ways will be put to death, as she will be. For I know this, you will be judged by your deeds, both good and bad. But to those who have not followed her teachings and have repented, or overcome their sins, I will make them rules over the nations.

They were impenitent, which means they did not repent. That tells us that they violated God's laws and didn't consider it to be a sin, so they never felt the need to repent. Why didn't they consider what they did to be a sin? They did what they did because they were deceived by following their Church Doctrines to reject God's law and to worship the Trinity. And that made them presumptuous sinners who were practicing lawlessness.

Jesus said, "**He who has an ear, let him hear what the Spirit says to the churches**." If you have ears (as all people do), listen to these words they are meant for all people! He wasn't just speaking to the church in Thyatira, he was speaking to you and me.

**Sardis** (Revelation 3:1-6) - the church thought it was alive with the doing of God's will, but it was dead. The message is to examine our deeds according to God's will (His word) and where we sometimes fail, we must repent, and it's still not too late. Hold fast to the message of God which you have received, before it is too late. Yet only a few will be saved, walking in Jesus' teachings ('**walk with me**'), having righteous deeds ('**clothed in white**') and have repented of their sins ('**unsoiled**'). Those who repent, or overcome their sins will be dressed in white and their names will not be blotted out of the Book of Life. Acts 3:19, "**Repent therefore and be converted, that your sins may be blotted out, so that times of refreshing may come from the presence of the Lord.**"

This church reminds me of those in Matthew 7:22, "**Many will say to Me in that day, 'Lord, Lord, have we not prophesied in Your name, cast out demons in Your name, and done many wonders in Your name?**". They called Jesus, 'Lord, Lord', and boasted about all the good things they did' in Jesus' name, they were very religious Christians, but yet they were rejected at the Gates of Heaven because they 'practiced lawlessness'. The Christian Church teaches today that we don't need to keep the laws of God, or His commandments – and thus they practice lawlessness.

I know many Christians will say, my church doesn't teach lawlessness. All Christians are lawless by their continual breaking of YHVH's First Commandment. Exodus 20:2-3, "**I am YHVH your God, who brought you out of the land of Egypt, out of the house of bondage, you shall have no other gods before Me.**" YHVH's First Commandment tells us to worship YHVH alone, and no Christian does that, because all Christians worship the Trinity. That alone makes them all lawless. There also the Sabbath law, most Christian violate, and most all Christian eat ham and other unclean meats.

Jesus said, "**He who has an ear, let him hear what the Spirit says to the churches.**" If you have ears (as all people do), listen to these words they are meant for all people! He wasn't just speaking to the church in Sardis, he was speaking to you and me.

**Philadelphia** (Revelation 3:7-13) Some of the people in the church were doing well and keeps Jesus' words. Like most churches today, there are the faithful few believers while most are lawless (synagogue of Satan) and this church is no different. God says that the false believers will someday serve the true believers. Those in the church who have kept the commandments of God, God will keep them from trials that the rest of humanity will suffer. God does not need to test them, for they have already been tested and have passed. God reminds them to hang on to their faith, or they could lose their crown of life. And for those that repent, or overcome their sin, God says that they will be like a pillar in His temple, in the New Jerusalem.

Before God wraps up the letters to the church, He adds hope, encouragement, and instruction to those who are persevering in the faith of Jesus. In their midst are those who are lawless (synagogue of Satan), and promise them a crown of life if they will preserver.

Jesus said, "**He who has an ear, let him hear what the Spirit says to the churches.**" If you have ears (as all people do), listen to these words they are meant for all people! He wasn't just speaking to the church in Philadelphia, he was speaking to you and me.

**Laodicea,** (Revelation 3:14-22) –

A pastor I knew went around a Minneapolis suburb asking people if they thought they are saved and going to heaven when they die. About 95% said 'yes', but when he asked them what they based their confidence on, only 5% of them responded with a Biblical answer of some sort. 95% that were confident of going to heaven had no 'scriptural' reason for believing that, other than they thought that they were good people. So, they were Laodicea, they were spiritually wretched, miserable, poor, blind, and naked and didn't' know it.

## ARE WE LAODICEA TODAY?

Many Bible scholars identify the seven churches in Revelation with seven historical periods of time in the church age. A careful study will show striking similarities of these seven churches to the churches at the historical periods that they represent. If that is true, and I believe it is, we are the church of Laodicea, the seventh and last church. Read below and see if the description doesn't fits like a glove.

Revelation 3:14-16,19, **"And to the angel of the church of the Laodiceans write, 'These things says the Amen, the Faithful and True Witness, the Beginning of the creation of God: "I know your works, that you are neither cold nor hot. I could wish you were cold or hot. So then, because you are lukewarm, and neither cold nor hot, I will vomit you out of My mouth. ... As many as I love, I rebuke and chasten. Therefore be zealous and repent."**

The Laodiceans were called lukewarm because their attitude toward God and God's law – was indifference. Being deceived by Christian Church doctrines, they were told that they didn't need to keep God's laws. Yet, they were nice and kind people, who kept some of God's laws, but they would not fully submit to YHVH's Divine authority. They were lukewarm in their commitment to YHVH God.

We know that keeping the law was a problem for them, because Jesus said (in verse 15) **"I know your works'**. And then in verse 19 he tells them the remedy for their problem; **"As many as I love, I rebuke and chasten. Therefore be zealous and repent."** There would be no other reason to **rebuke, chasten,** and call for them to **repent and be zealous'** unless they were presumptuous (unrepentant) sinners. Being '**lukewarm**' tells us that they only kept some of God's laws but not all of them. They, like most Christians, had a 'warm' veneer of righteousness on the outside, attending church and doing 'good' things, but they were 'lukewarm' rebels at heart, rejecting some (or all) of God's law, and thereby rejecting God's authority over them. To reject even one of God's laws, is to rebel against God's authority. Jesus had to tell them to be zealous for God and His law because they were not - they had only half heartily kept some of God's Laws, the rest they rejected or set aside – believing that the laws were not for them. Perhaps they were told that they are not under the law by their church doctrines, and being religious they follow the instruction of their church doctrines.

Revelation 3:17-18, **"Because you say, 'I am rich, have become wealthy, and have need of nothing'—and do not know that you are wretched, miserable, poor, blind, and naked— 18 I counsel you to buy from Me gold refined in the fire, that you may be rich; and white garments, that you may be clothed,** *that* **the shame of your nakedness may not be revealed; and anoint your eyes with eye salve, that you may see."**

The first problem was that they don't know their true condition. They think that they are well off, but Jesus said, 'no', just the opposite is true. It seems that deception has caused them to be confused about what it takes to be acceptable to God. Perhaps someone, like Paul, told them that it was OK to reject God's commandments, saying "Surely you will not die", so 'just believe'.

The condition of the Laodicea church is that they are wretched, miserable, poor, blind, and naked – while they thought that they were rich, wealthy and in need of nothing. They were seriously deceived about their condition. This, of course, is speaking of their spiritual condition; they were spiritually wretched, spiritually miserable, spiritually poor, spiritually blind and spiritually naked.

Being spiritually poor means that they were spiritually lacking in their righteousness. <u>Spiritually miserable</u> means that they were to be pitied for their spiritual condition. And they were <u>spiritually</u> <u>wretched</u>, because they didn't even know their desperate spiritual condition. And they were <u>spiritually blind</u> because they had no spiritual discernment to know it, and thus they didn't even know that they were lacking. In other words they were comfortable in their lost condition, confident of their assumed salvation while they were lost, they had a false assurance of heaven – yet they were naked of a robe of righteousness. According to 2John 2:11, spiritual blindness is the same as walking in darkness of sin (lawlessness). That's why they were spiritually naked of a robe of righteousness. Why were they in such a miserable condition? Could it be that their spiritual leaders convinced them that they could be saved and lawless at the same time? It seems as though they were told that it was OK to set God's laws aside because "salvation is by grace", but is that true even for the lawless?

The lawless are those have rejected some, or all of God's laws, figuring that somehow those laws don't apply to them, and thus they are <u>spiritually poor</u>. Having been deceived into rejecting God's law(s), and worshiping the Trinity, they don't see the violation of the rejected law(s) as sin, so they are <u>spiritually blind.</u> So now they are sinners who don't even know that they are sinners, they are <u>spiritually wretched</u>, and feeling no need for repentance, so they will never repent, they are <u>spiritually miserable</u> and therefore <u>naked</u> of all righteousness. This Laodicea condition is a description of presumptuous sinners who have reject some, or all, of God's laws, and so when they violate the rejected law(s) they don't consider it to be a sin, and therefore they will never repent – so they are 'defiled' with sin. But, they kept enough of God's laws to look moral in man's eyes, however the outright rejection of just one of God's laws makes a person a rebel in God's eyes. Doesn't that sounds like the lawless Christian 'church' of today? According to the Christian Church doctrines, it's OK to be lawless, but according to God's standard that is a fatal condition, apart from true repentance.

## **NOT MY CHURCH**

You may be saying, that's not my church, we keep God's commandment. Do you keep all Ten of the Ten Commandments? Do you keep the Sabbath (4th commandment)? Do you worship YHVH alone (1st Commandment)? Do you keep God's commandment which forbids the eating of pork, shrimp, lobster, or meat with its blood in it? Do you keep the Biblical Holy Days; Passover, Pentecost, Trumpets, Yom Kipper and Tabernacles? If you can answer 'yes' to these questions, you are doing well – and you are not in a Christian Church. If you answered 'no' to any of these questions, and don't know that you need to repent, you have been deceived and you are spiritually poor, blind, miserable and wretched. (The Scriptures tell us that if we don't keep these laws, and if we were judged today we would be among the lost lawless, who need to repent.) For rejecting even one of God's laws is an act of rebellion against His Divine authority, and that will cause us to fall under His judgment – the judgment of a jealous God who is a consuming fire.

It was their spiritually blindness, which resulted in Laodicea's nakedness – naked of all righteousness. Their blindness was because they were walking contrary to God's law – they were walking in darkness because they had no light – and therefore lacked any righteousness. Those in Laodicea were naked of righteousness, that is, they lacked 'the robe of righteousness' that they should have had to cover their sinful nakedness. Lamentation 1:8 (ESV), **"Jerusalem sinned grievously; therefore she became filthy; all who honored her despise her, for they have seen her nakedness; she herself groans and turns her face away."** To be 'naked' is to lack righteousness. The robe they needed is defined a few chapters later in Revelation 19:7-8, **"Let us be glad and rejoice and give Him glory, for the marriage of the Lamb has come, and His wife has made herself ready."** And to her it was granted to be arrayed in fine linen, clean and bright, for the fine linen is the righteous acts of the saints."** The fine linen robe that Laodicea was missing was the **'righteous acts of the saints'**, i.e., keeping the Commandments of God.

Righteousness according to Jesus in Matthew 5:17-20, according to Luke 1:6, and according to Moses words in Deuteronomy 6:25 - is keeping the law of God – that is being right with God. Laodicea apparently had no righteousness, because they didn't walk in the light of God's word and keep His law. In that respect, Laodicea is a mirror image of the Christian church of today, telling and convincing people that there is no need to keep God's law, they say it's been done away at the cross. So the people reject God's laws and live in sin, assuming they are saved by 'cheap grace', and not even knowing that they are lost – and being told, **'surely you will not die'**. They are **'wretched, miserable, poor, blind, and naked'**.

God told Laodicea that they needed to see their own condition, and gain for themselves a robe of righteousness. If they don't, He will vomit them out because of their lawlessness (Revelation 3:16) just as He vomited Israel out of the land because of their lawlessness (Leviticus 18:24-28). Woe to the shepherds who teach others to be lawless – theirs will be the greater condemnation.

That same problem was an issue in Jeremiah's time, with the religious leaders. Lamentations 2:14, **"Your prophets have seen for you false and deceptive visions; They have not uncovered your iniquity, To bring back your captives, But have envisioned for you false prophecies and delusions."** The religious leaders were teaching people falsely and did '**not uncover the people's sins'**. The religious leaders were indifferent to the law of God and indifferent on how people violated it, we could say that they were lawless teachers who were teaching people to be lawless. What has changed today? The religious leaders (Jeremiah 6:14) said, '**peace, peace'**, telling people that everything is fine, there's nothing to worry about, your salvation is secure – while the people are lawless and condemned. And the same message is going out of the pulpits today. Lawless and sinful people are told, as Eve was told, you can be lawless and **"surely you will not die"**. And they are told just 'believe in Jesus', say the sinner's prayer, 'plead the blood', 'trust in the cross' and then God will be pleased – and everything is OK – they say 'peace, peace', when it is not. In most cases the religious leaders aren't evil, just deceived, and teaching what their 'church denomination' requires them to teach.

The bottom line for those in Laodicea is this, Revelation 3:19, **"As many as I love, I rebuke and chasten. Therefore be zealous and repent."** Those in Laodicea will receive God's rebuke and chastening, but that is from a loving God in effort to get them to **"be zealous and repent"**. '**Repent**' of course means to commit or re-commit ourselves to submit to God's Divine authority, so that we stop what we are doing and go the other way. The fruit of repentance is that we stop breaking God's law and start keeping it. But in connection with repenting of our lawlessness, God told them to be '**zealous**'. We might ask, zealous for what? I believe that we can know that by reading Acts 21:20, **"And when they heard it, they glorified the Lord. And they said to him, "You see, brother, how many myriads of Jews there are who have believed, and they are all zealous for the law"**. These early Christians who we read about in the Book of Acts were described as Jews that were zealous for the Law of God. To be zealous means that they were eager and willing to learn of God's law and to keep it – and that dovetails perfectly with the command to '**repent**'. Is this a message needed in our church today? Absolutely, because today's church is **wretched, miserable, poor, blind, and naked** – while they are deceived into thinking that they are rich, wealthy and in need of nothing!

Revelation 3: 20-22, **"Behold, I stand at the door and knock. If anyone hears My voice and opens the door, I will come in to him and dine with him, and he with Me. To him who overcomes I will grant to sit with Me on My throne, as I also overcame and sat down with My Father on His throne.**
**"He who has an ear, let him hear what the Spirit says to the churches."**

When we knock on Heaven's door, it means that we are seeking to communicate with God by prayer. For Jesus to knock on our door means that he wants to communicate with us. How does he do that? He does that through his word, that is, his teachings as recorded in the New Testament. What does it mean to '**hear**' Jesus voice and '**open the door**'? John 10:27, "**My sheep hear My voice, and I know them, and they follow Me.**" It means to hear and obey his teachings as we read in the Gospels – Jesus' teachings and commands were for us to keep God's law (Matthew 5:17-19, John 14:15-21, Revelation 12:17, 14:12, 22:14), to worship YHVH the Father alone (Matthew 4:10, John 4:22-23, John 17:3), to pray to the YHVH Father alone (Matthew 6:8-13), and seeking forgiveness from YHVH the Father alone (Matthew 6:14-15). What does it mean that he will come in and dine with us? John 14:23-24, "**Jesus answered and said to him, "If anyone loves Me, he will keep My word; and My Father will love him, and We will come to him and make Our home with him. He who does not love Me does not keep My words; and the word which you hear is not Mine but the Father's who sent Me.**" It means fellowship, friendship, and it means that God will love us and we will receive God's saving grace – which He gives to those who love Him and keep His commandments, those are who He loves (Exodus 20:6, John14:21) and he will dine with.

Laodicea is the current Christian Church that Jesus is rebuking and calling to repent – because they have turned away from Jesus' words and teachings. But in reality, in rejecting Jesus' teachings they are rejecting the words of God the Father (YHVH) which He gave to Jesus to speak. So Jesus and his teachings are rejected by the Christian church, and the Father is rejected with him.

The lawless Christian Church is much like the Prodigal son. Having rejected his father's rules and laws, the Prodigal son, after a short while, became wretched, miserable, poor, blind, and naked. What the Prodigal son became physically, the Christian church has become spiritually by rejecting the 'law and prophets' the church is living in the filth of rebellion, sin and lawlessness. How did the son recover from being wretched, miserable, poor, blind, and naked? He saw the error of his ways, then he humbled himself and returned to father, even offer to be a servant who would necessarily obey all of the commands of the father. The prodigal son submitted himself to the father as his supreme authority. And that's the message that Jesus wants us to see here. Instead of rebelling against YHVH God's laws and commands, we need to submit to His Divine authority.

## **CONCLUSION**

Where are the seven churches today? They are heaps of rubble. Their lamps stands have been removed because they rejected, or ignore the Spirit's message to them.

It's also very clear by looking at Christianity that it is certainly not ready for Jesus' return. I fear for those that call themselves Christians on Judgment Day. They are not even coming close to living as God, or Jesus, have called us to live. Although almost all in the church think they are saved by what they believe, their church membership or by church sacraments. Since they have been deceived by the Church doctrines they don't know that they are sinners, so they won't seek their own righteousness by repenting of their sins - and yet they are anxiously waiting for Jesus, even praying for his soon return! They are hopelessly lost, wretched, poor, blind and naked, and they will be turned away at the gates of Heaven because they didn't enter the narrow gate of 'Repentance' which would have led them to travel the narrow road of obedience to God's laws. So they will hear Jesus say, 'Depart from me, you who practice lawlessness'.

Yes, the 'many' are deceived and you may say it's not their fault for the Church, the priests and pastors have deceived them. But yet, are they not responsible for using the resources available to them to seek out the truth for themselves? Will they be responsible for what they know and also for what they should know? Is willfully ignorant going to be a valid excuse on Judgment Day? Can we Justify ignorance when Bibles are plentiful and available to all? According to Matthew 7:13-14, all on the Broad way were deceived, yet their final end is eternal destruction. So it appears that just because they are deceived does not mean that God's will automatically forgive them. But, thankfully, God is the judge.

A few hundred years ago, Bibles were scarce, or only the rich could afford them, and even then, not everyone could read. But today, do have we any valid excuses for not knowing what God said, and obeying it?

Some people are willing to be deceived, perhaps because they really don't want to keep God's law anyway, so if anyone can assure them that God doesn't expect them to keep His law, they are all too happy to accept that teaching.

But now that you have read this book you know better. Please respond in a way that will glorify God. And pray that God will open the eyes of the spiritually "**wretched, miserable, poor, blind, and naked**" Laodiceans – that they may see the truth and cloth themselves with their own righteousness before Judgment Day.

In closing this letter to the Laodicea Church Jesus says in Revelation 3:20, **"Behold, I stand at the door and knock. If anyone hears My voice and opens the door, I will come in to him and dine with him, and he with Me."** The picture is that Jesus is currently not in their hearts. He is not currently their lord whom they obey and listen to – and that's why they are having the spiritual troubles they are having. But here Jesus is telling them, and us, that if we will hear his voice and act on it, i.e., obey him, he will come in and dine with us. Of course the dining part is figurative. In the ancient world you didn't invite strangers to come in and dine with you, only close friends, and family. To dine with someone was to express a close and personal relationship. That's why the Pharisee accused Jesus thus, Luke 15:2, "**And the Pharisees and scribes complained, saying, "This Man receives sinners and eats with them."** And it was astonishing that Judas would betray Jesus after dining with him, Mark 14:18, "**Now as they sat and ate, Jesus said, "Assuredly, I say to you, one of you who eats with Me will betray Me."** Jesus is telling us that when we obey him that we will enter into a personal and close relationship with him – and being that judgment was given to him, and that could be a very important issue on Judgment Day. In John 8:52 we read, "'**If anyone keeps My word he shall never taste death."** To keep Jesus' word is to obey the Father and keep His commandments.

Jesus said, "**He who has an ear, let him hear what the Spirit says to the churches**." If you have ears (as all people do), listen to these words because they are meant for all people! Jesus wasn't just speaking to the church in Laodicea, he was speaking to you and me.

## SUMMARY OF CHURCH MESSAGES

The earliest worshiper of God, who believed Jesus to be the messiah continued in their Jewish synagogues, practicing their faith as Jesus had commanded (Acts 24:14). The 'church' was perfect, as it was under the leadership of Jesus' Apostles and disciples. Then along comes Paul. Paul created a new breed of 'Christians'. Paul converted them to Judaism but told them it wasn't necessary to keep God's laws (Acts 21:18-21). These lawless ones soon separated themselves for the faithful Jews, and started Christian Churches. In time their Jewishness disappeared and they embraced Paul's words as the Gospel truth, and the doctrine of the Trinity.

God's message to the churches could be condensed into; Keep the commandments of God, and Jesus' words (testimony), be careful that you are not led into lawlessness by a deceiver, such as Jezebel, Balaam, false believers, a Church, or the Nicolaitans. Repent when you fail and God will accept you back as He did the Prodigal Son. Overcomers (who overcome their sin and sinful ways) are promised eternal life, rulership over kingdoms, eating hidden manna, eating from the tree of life, receiving a new name, getting a white stone, etc.

At the end of each church letter we read the phrase, "**He who has an ear, let him hear what the Spirit says to the churches."** '**The Spirit**' or the '**Holy Spirit**' is God's breath from which He utters His words of the letter to that church. God's Sprit is 'His word' the 'Scriptures'. The Greek word for 'hearing' also means heeding.

The intent of the letters for each church is that the letters weren't just for those who belonged to that specific church in the specific time in history, the message is for all people in all time periods.

## PAUL'S CHURCHES?

It is interesting to note that in the Book of the Revelation, the seven letters were written to the seven churches were primarily letters to rebuke and correct what was going on in the Churches. And notice that all seven churches are in that land of Asia-minor, which today we call Turkey. And all seven churches were founded by Paul. Jesus told those seven churches if they didn't repent, he'd remove their lamps, and all seven churches have failed to exist to this day. Their lamps have been removed. However, there is no letters to the churches outside of Turkey – which Jesus' Apostles founded. And, history tells us that Israel had a number of churches, yet they had no received a Revelation letter by Jesus, and there were also churches in Egypt and as far away as India which received no Revelation letter by Jesus. It seems that it was only Churches that Paul founded the received letters of corrections. It seems that the other churches, which were not founded by Paul, didn't encounter the same theological errors that Paul introduced to those seven Asia-minor churches, mainly lawlessness and a skewed idea of who Jesus was?

Paul's Seven Churches all failed, but unfortunately his epistles survived and were instruments for his lawless theology to infect all the rest of Christianity. The Christian Church is the Broad Way of lawlessness leading to destruction. Those who escape it are the Few on the Narrow Way to God's Kingdom.

End of Chapter

## CHAPTER 3 – SIX SEALS AND FOUR HORSES

## THE FOUR HORSES OF THE APOCALYPSE

Verses 1-8 (NKJV)– "**And I looked, and behold, a white horse. He who sat on it had a bow; and a crown was given to him, and he went out conquering and to conquer.**
3 When He opened the second seal, I heard the second living creature saying, "Come and see." 4 Another horse, fiery red, went out. And it was granted to the one who sat on it to take peace from the earth, and that people should kill one another; and there was given to him a great sword.
5 When He opened the third seal, I heard the third living creature say, "Come and see." So I looked, and behold, a black horse, and he who sat on it had a pair of scales in his hand. 6 And I heard a voice in the midst of the four living creatures saying, "A quart of wheat for a denarius, and three quarts of barley for a denarius; and do not harm the oil and the wine."
7 When He opened the fourth seal, I heard the voice of the fourth living creature saying, "Come and see." 8 So I looked, and behold, a pale horse. And the name of him who sat on it was Death, and Hades followed with him. And power was given to them over a fourth of the earth, to kill with sword, with hunger, with death, and by the beasts of the earth."

We read about four horses: white, red, black and pale.

The Christian religion practiced in the world today is not the same Christian religion that was practiced by early church, known as 'The Way'. We read about the belief and practices of 'The Way' in Acts 24:14, "**But this I confess to you, that according to the Way which they call a sect, so I worship the God** *(YHVH)* **of my fathers, believing** *(or committing to)* **all things which are written in the Law and in the Prophets.**". "The Way" practiced according to the instructions of Jesus' first generation disciples, those who trained directly under Jesus and his Apostles. The Christian religion has then mutated over the centuries from a pure white horse of the earliest church, to different stages: persecutions (blood red horse), dark ages caused by a lack of 'light' of God's word (black horse), until it ends with the pale horse of death. That's where the Christian Church is today....all who have, and are practicing their Christian faith according to the lawless and idolatrous Church doctrines are in a spiritual dead church and they will receive eternal death following the judgment.

## THE DEATH OF CHRISTIANITY

According to the grey horse (the color of death), death is Christianity's final and current state. Christianity spiritually died when it accepted the Doctrine of the Trinity because it no longer worships and serves the one true God. That's when Christianity died in YHVH God's eyes.

How could Christianity accept that non-biblical doctrine. The Roman Church, then and today, believes that its authority is above that of the Bible. So its doctrines do not need to Biblical, logical, or to even make sense, they are simply decreed to be doctrines by the Church.

## CONCLUSION

So, after the Seven Churches and the Four Horses, they Christian church is not mentioned again, except under the title Babylon the Great. From this point forward God calls His people to come out of that corrupt system of Babylon the Great and He release His plague on those who stay in it.

## CHAPTER 4 – THE THREE ANGEL'S MESSAGES

### REVELATION CHAPTER 14

If I could only choose only one Book of the Bible, I would choose the Book of the Revelation. I know that's perhaps kind of an odd choice, but I would choose it because it is YHVH God's last message to mankind and so it is full of pertinent information including His final instructions and His final warnings. In His last message He wanted to make sure that everything was clear and there were no misconceptions about the way and means of salvation. This book was the last book written and it was written after the Gospels and the Epistles, so it addresses any erroneous perceptions that may have resulted from a misunderstanding of those writings.

The Book of the Revelation is like a capstone on a structure, or the frosting on a cake, because contains God's last warnings and instructions as well as revealing what went wrong with the 'Christian Church' and why it became known as 'Babylon the Great' and it reveals how and why we must get out of Babylon before the plagues. In this book we also learn what happens to those who stay in Babylon. And much of that is all is in Chapter 14 of the Book of the Revelation. That's the one Chapter that I would choose if I had to choose a single chapter, and after you read this, you will understand why I would chose Chapter 14. So, we need to study this chapter above all others in the Book of the Revelation, and perhaps in the New Testament.

In the previous chapters (2 and 3) God has revealed how the Christian Church has spiritually fallen. Those messages were given in letters to seven churches established by Paul. The Christian Church became progressively more and more corrupt, worldly, and compromised, as it turned away from God's word to embrace the words and dictates of man, and now the Christian Church is a dead church, "**wretched, miserable, poor, blind, and naked**". And again we see the same church history in the Four horses; beginning with a pure white horse which was the earliest apostolic church. Then it was red with the blood of persecution, and then it turned black. The blackness is it lost the light of God's word, in the dark ages. And without the light of God's word, the Church died (that is the pale or gray horse is the color of death).

The early leaders of the Christian Church, following the Apostolic era, drawing their theology from Paul's epistles were deceived into embracing Paul's lawless teachings. Virtually all of Christianity today is following Paul's thinking and have rejected the need to keep YHVH's laws, the entire Christian Church has been deceived just as the Serpent beast deceived Eve. Then, in the Church's continued degradation, the church compromised its teachings about

God by allowing the incorporation of the 'sun-god trinity' in to the Christian Church. The Christian Church made 'lawlessness' and the 'worship of the Trinity' into doctrines of the Church. And so, lawlessness and the worship the Trinity are deceptions that continue to deceive all of those who call themselves Christians. And thus, 'All of the world is deceived and wonders after the beast..' (Revelation 12:9-13:3).

It's because of those deceptions, that beginning in Chapter 14, God is starts referring to the Christian Church as 'Babylon the Great' and He is calling people out of Babylon to be among the redeemed, so that they may avoid the plagues which are about to be poured out.

## **THE CHRISTIAN CHURCH IS BABYLON**

The Book of the Revelation will clearly show us that today's Christian Church is Babylon the Great. Babylon is a known for its defiance of God, and the Christian Church is in defiance of God. The First and most important Commandment is found in Exodus 20:2-3, **"I am YHVH your God, who brought you out of the land of Egypt, out of the house of bondage, you shall have no other gods before Me."** YHVH God demands that we worship Him alone, yet the Christian Church defiantly refuses and instead they worship a trinity of gods. According to the Scriptures Jesus spoke YHVH's words with YHVH's authority and told us to worship YHVH alone (Matthew 4:10), but the church defiantly refuses.

There are many more cases of defiance, such as an 'Easter Sunday Ham Dinner', which rejects God's Passover which He told us to keep forever, and it's a rejection of God's Sabbath to keep Sunday instead and it is a rejection of God's dietary laws. But yet all of the Church's issues of defiance pale in the shadow of the gross violation of the First Commandment. If we fail on the First Commandment we are idolaters and it really doesn't matter what other commandments we have keep or violated. Violating the First Commandment alone is enough to classify the Christian Church as Babylonian idolaters. But there is much more as you will read.

Worshiping the Trinity dishonors YHVH God by violating His First Commandment. Worshiping the Trinity dishonors YHVH God by is taking glory, honor, praise and worship away from YHVH God and giving it to another, and that is spiritual fornication, spiritual adultery, and idolatry. Babylon, the Christian Church, will be judged for her spiritual fornications (Revelation 14:8, 17:2,4, 18:3,9, 19:2) in worshiping the Trinity.

Babylon doesn't show up in Book of the Revelation until after the 4 horses, and the 7 churches are described. The four horses are a quick summary of the Church history; from a pure white apostolic church, which became red with persecuted, and then, over the centuries, manmade laws, doctrines, and traditions replaced the light of God's word and the church became the black horse with the lack of the light of God's word, and that resulted in it becoming the pale horse of spiritual death (Pale or gray, is a mixture of black and white, or lukewarm, like the dead church of Laodicea). In today's Christian church lawlessness prevails, and again, the 'lawless' are not those who are completely evil and sin every chance they get. Lawlessness means that they have set aside one or more of God's laws and they ignore them and then violate them at will, not even considering it to be a sin so there's no though of repentance. A lawless person may attend church weekly and from all appearances a very nice and religious person and perhaps they keep 99% of God's laws, but in that 1% they will not keep, they are spurning God's Divine authority. In that rebellion against God's authority they are looking Him the eye and defiantly saying, 'No, I will not do that'.

People are usually lawless because they have been deceived by church doctrines into thinking that some, or all, of God's laws are obsolete, out-of-date, done away with, nailed to the cross, and that we are not under the jurisdiction of God's law.

Those who are deceived by the Christian Church into practicing lawlessness, and according to the Scriptures, will receive eternal death.

In Revelation 2 and 3 we read a more detailed account of the spiritual history of the Church, divided into seven parts – which are each associated with one of the seven churches. The Seven Churches again start off the good apostolic church, then persecution happens, and then the next churches become compromised and corruption sets in, as God's laws are replaced with manmade teachings, and the churches spiritually degrade until the final lawless Laodicea church–keeps some of God's laws and ignores the rest, making them lukewarm. Laodicea being lukewarm in regards to God's commands, is the final step on the migration path from a pure white church to complete lawlessness. Being lukewarm is being deceived into believing that it's not important to keep YHVH's laws, so they have an indifferent the attitude towards God's law. Then, for the rest of the Book of the Revelation the church becomes known as Babylon the Great. That's why we only read about Babylon the Great in the Book of the Revelation after the seven churches and the four horses, and then church is no longer mentioned as a religion.

## **THE REDEEMED – HOW TO BE ONE OF THEM…**

Beginning in the first four verses of this Chapter we will find out who will be redeemed and who will not be redeemed by identifying some unique characteristics about each group. Verses 1-4, (NKJV) **"Then I looked, and behold, a Lamb standing on Mount Zion, and with Him one hundred *and* forty-four thousand, having His Father's name written in their foreheads. 2 And I heard a voice from heaven, like the voice of many waters, and like** the voice of loud thunder. And I heard the sound of harpists playing their harps. 3 They sang as it were a new song before the throne, before the four living creatures, and the elders; and no one could learn that song except the hundred *and* forty-four thousand <u>who were redeemed from the earth.</u> 4 These are the ones who were <u>not defiled with women</u>, for they are virgins. These are the ones who <u>follow the Lamb wherever He goes</u>. These were redeemed from *among* men, *being* firstfruits to God and to the Lamb."

The number 144,000, which is probably a symbolic number, represent the number of those that "**were redeemed from the earth**" (vs. 3) – the redeemed are all of those who were saved from eternal destruction. What do we know about this group? They all have the Father's Name, '**Yahoveh**' or **YHVH**', written in their foreheads – literally on the frontal lobe of the brain. The frontal lobe is the decision maker for the brain, (I know that many translations say 'on the forehead' but the Greek really says 'in the forehead').

God's name in the forehead is the 'seal' of God. The seal identifies their ownership and as a seal seals up a book, or scroll, so their fate is sealed, they are redeemed. They belong to YHVH God because that's whom they worship, – they don't worship Jesus or the Trinity. Verse 3 says that the redeemed had harps and sang a new song. We see the same images in Psalm 33 where is says the righteous sang a new song of praise to YHVH with harps and shouts of joy. (What is a 'New Song'?, see below).

Then in verse 4 we read that the redeemed were not '**defiled with women**'. A woman, in Bible prophesy is a religious organization, or a church – there are a number of 'women' in this Book. There is the 'Great Whore' who is the Roman Catholic Church and her many harlot daughters, who are the Protestant Churches (together that's all of Christianity). Those who were not redeemable were defiled by the 'women', for we know that those who were redeemed (the 144,000) were undefiled by the 'women'. What was it about the 'women' that defiled people? It was the Christian Church doctrines that caused people to sin, and not seek forgiveness through repentant. They were defiled with unrepentant sin.

What is the defilement? First let's look to see what it means to be '**defiled**'. Zechariah 3:4 tells us that filthy garments are iniquities, or sins. Psalm 119:1, helps us understand what it means be defiled, it says, "**Blessed are the undefiled in the way, Who walk in the Torah of YHVH**". Isaiah 24:5a, "**The earth is also defiled under its inhabitants, Because they have transgressed the laws (Torah)…**". So to be defiled is to transgress God's laws, or God's Torah, and that is 'sin' according to 1John 3:4. And those who continue in sin without repentance are those who are practicing lawlessness. Matthew 13:41-42 says at the end of time, God will send out His angels to gather those who practiced lawlessness and cast them into a fiery furnace.

The 144,000 avoided being defiled with corrupt church doctrines. What was that defilement which was caused by corrupt Christian church doctrine? Those who are undefiled are those that walk in the ways of the Torah, God's law. So those that do not walk in the ways of God's Torah law, are those that are defiled. Those who follow the ways of the 'women' (i.e. Church Doctrine) which tell us that we don't need to keep God's laws, because; we are saved by grace, and the laws were nailed to the cross, Old Covenant, just a tutor, fading away, they are bondage, they are obsolete, out-of-date, etc. Those who then set aside some or all of God's laws are practicing lawlessness and are defiled with unrepentant sin, and have filthy garments.

In contrast to those who were defiled by the lawless doctrines of churches (women), are those who reject those Christian Church doctrines and instead they '**follow the Lamb wherever he goes**'. That is they accepted Jesus' teachings instead of the teachings of the lawless Christian Church doctrines. Jesus told us to keep the '**law and the Prophets**' and **worship YHVH** alone – thus they are no defiled and have YHVH written in their foreheads. The redeemed follow the teachings of the Lamb. Those who didn't do that are the defiled and will receive the mark of the beast. Which means the entire Christian Church will receive the Mark of the Beast, unless they come out of Babylon to be redeemed. God pleads with Christians, "Come out of her My people".

While Jesus (the Lamb) told us to keep the 'law and the Prophets', the Christian Church has ignored that, and it uses Paul's lawless teachings to create their lawless church doctrines. Convincing people that they don't need to keep God's 'law and the Prophets', telling them that the Jesus did away with the law, he nailed it to the cross, and because he died on the cross we are saved 'grace through faith apart from the law', etc. So they believe that they can live a lawless lifestyle and won't suffer any consequences, and they can still be saved inspite for their lawlessness. (Isn't that exactly what the Serpent told Eve?). Those who accept and practice any of the corrupt Christian Church doctrines are '**defiled with women**'. However, anyone could be cleansed by true repentance, and returning to God's Torah law, but unfortunately, the deceived feel no need of it, because they have chosen a different supreme authority-believing Paul instead of Jesus.

How many defiled (lawless) people do you suppose YHVH God will allow into His Kingdom? Absolutely none. God promises His kingdom will be one of peace, joy, harmony, and love – a lawless person is not compatible with that. God demonstrated the lawless will not be allowed in paradise when He evicted Adam and Eve.

But wait, aren't we free from the Law? Yes, Paul said we are free from the law, the law is dead, nailed to the cross, it's done away with, and we died to the demands, it was a temporary tutor, it is bondage, and the condemnation of the law. But is that what did Jesus taught? Paul's teachings must be made to conform to Jesus' teachings, not the other way around. After all, whose authority do you submit, Jesus (God's word made flesh) or Paul? If there is a conflict between the two, which one do you consider the greater authority? It has to be Jesus. And what did Jesus' personally trained inner circle, Peter, James, and John to teach? And what did the early apostolic church, which was pastor'ed by Jesus' apostles, teach and practice?

**Peter** - We hear from Peter in 2Peter 3:16-17, "**as also in all his epistles, "speaking in them of these things, in which are some things hard to understand, which untaught and unstable *people* twist to their own destruction, as *they do* also the rest of the Scriptures. You therefore, beloved, since you know *this* beforehand, beware lest you also fall from your own steadfastness, being led away with the error of the wicked** *(or lawless)*" ; Peter said that if you understand Paul in a way that leads you to believe that you can be lawless and still be saved, you have misunderstood Paul. Peter said that a lawless understanding will lead to your destruction. **John** - John said, (1John 5:3),"**For this is the love of God, that we keep His commandments. And His commandments are not burdensome.**" John said that we need to keep the Law of God, and he told us that sin is 'lawlessness' (1John 3:4). There were those at John's time that said since there is no longer a law, there is no longer sin. John told them, "**If we say that we have no sin, we deceive ourselves, and the truth is not in us**" (1John 1:18). **James** - James wrote, (James 2:20), "**But do you want to know, O foolish man, that faith without works is dead?**" So James said that we must have good works (keeping the commandments) to validate our faith. James 1:22, "**But be doers of the word, and not hearers only, deceiving yourselves.**" **The Apostolic church** - What did the earliest church teach? Acts 20:21,"**And when they heard *it,* they glorified the Lord. And they said to him, "You see, brother, how many myriads of Jews there are who have believed, and they are all zealous for the law**". So those who followed the Apostles teachings kept the law of God – they were even zealous for it. (How many Christians do you know that are 'zealous' for the law?) The apostolic church was called '**the Way**', and here is what they believed; (Acts 24:14); "**But this I confess to you, that according to 'the Way' which they call a sect, so I worship the God of my fathers, believing all things which are written in the Law and in the Prophets**." They worshiped YHVH, as their Jewish ancestral fathers did, and they "**believe all things written in the Law and in the Prophets**". 'The Way' was the earliest form of the Christian Church, which followed Jesus' teachings. That doesn't sound like they discarded God's law as the modern Church has, nor did they worship a Trinity.

And now let's look at what the greatest New Testament authority, **Jesus,** said (Matthew 5:17-20, "**Do not think that I came to destroy the Law or the Prophets. I did not come to destroy but to fulfill. 18 For assuredly, I say to** you, till heaven and earth pass away, one jot or one tittle will by no means pass from the law till all is fulfilled. 19 Whoever therefore breaks one of the least of these commandments, and teaches men so, shall be called least in the kingdom of heaven; but whoever does and teaches them, he shall be called great in the kingdom of heaven. 20 For I say to you, that unless your righteousness exceeds the righteousness of the scribes and Pharisees, you will by no means enter the kingdom of heaven.'**) Jesus said that we must keep the Law and the Prophets until heaven and earth pass away, for that's where our righteous comes from, and you will not enter the kingdom of heaven without that righteousness.  Then he said that the lawless will not enter heaven (Matthew 7:23, "**And then I will declare to them, 'I never knew you; depart from Me, you who practice lawlessness!'**") They will be utterly destroyed (Matthew 13:41-42, "**The Son of Man will send out His angels, and they will gather out of His kingdom all things that offend, and those who practice lawlessness, 42 and will cast them into the furnace of fire. There will be wailing and gnashing of teeth**".).  How serious was Jesus about us keeping God's law?  In Matthew 18:8-9, Jesus tells us that if our hand, foot or eye causes us to sin (break God's Law) we should cut it off, better to be missing a foot, hand or eye than to end up in hell (which, according to Jesus, is the consequences of breaking God's law – i.e., sin.)  In the Book of Revelation Jesus said that the saints (redeemed) are those that '**keep the commandments of God'** (Revelation 12:17), "**And the dragon was enraged with the woman, and he went to make war with the rest of her offspring, who keep the commandments of God and have the testimony of Jesus Christ**". Revelation 14:12, "**Here is the patience of the saints; here** *are* **those who keep the commandments of God and the faith of Jesus**" and according to Jesus, it's only those who keep the commandments of God that will eat from the tree of Life and enter the New Jerusalem (Revelation 22:14, "**Blessed** *are* **those who do His commandments, that they may have the right to the tree of life, and may enter through the gates into the city**.").  Revelation 22:14 was given to us as a final warning, in the last chapter of the last book of the Bible, heed its' warning. You can only practice a lawless lifestyle by rejecting God's law, rejecting the Prophets warnings and ignoring Jesus' repeated commands, teachings and warnings. As clear as this is, the 'church' refuses to tell people to keep the law of God. It's astonishing!  The Christian Church promotes lawlessness, including the violation of the First Commandment which commands us to worship YHVH alone.

So you will have to choose between following Jesus or following the Christian Church doctrines.  But remember that Revelation 14:4 said that those who were redeemed from the earth are those who followed the Lamb (Jesus) wherever he goes (i.e., obey him whatever it cost – wherever it leads them). Also remember also that Jesus said that it's by his words that we will be judged (John 12:48, "**He who rejects Me, and does not receive My words, has that which judges him—the word that I have spoken will judge him in the last day"). We better obey Jesus and keep the 'law and the prophets' and worship YHVH alone!

## THE REDEEMED SING A NEW SONG UNTO YHVH

When we prepare to sing a song unto YHVH our God, we generally go look for a song in the Church hymnal. Unfortunately, those are all old songs. They were written, sometimes more that hundred years ago, by people we never even heard of. When I look in the hymnal I often don't even know the words of those 'old songs' until I sing them – So how could those 'old songs' express my personal thoughts, feelings and experiences? The words of those 'old songs' were written to express the feelings of someone else's heart and mind, not mine. Singing those old songs is a religious ritual, but that's not true worship.

## WHAT YHVH OUR GOD WANTS OF US IS A 'NEW SONG'.

Psalm 40:3, "**He has put a new song in my mouth— Praise to our God; Many will see it and fear, And will trust in YHVH.**"

Psalms 68:4, "**Sing unto God, sing praises to his name: extol him that rides upon the heavens by his name YAH, and rejoice before him.**"

Psalm 96:1, "**Oh, sing to YHVH a new song! Sing to YHVH, all the earth.**"

Isaiah 42:10, "**Sing to YHVH a new song, And His praise from the ends of the earth, you who go down to the sea, and all that is in it, you coastlands and you inhabitants of them!**"

Revelation 14:3 "**They sang as it were a new song before the throne, before the four living creatures, and the elders; and no one could learn that song except the hundred and forty-four thousand who were redeemed from the earth.**"

According to Revelation 14:3 only the redeemed can sing that 'new song', because only they have learned it. How did they learn it? And what is a 'new song'?

First of all, a 'New Song' is always addressed to and about YHVH God, and Him alone. All of the redeemed have YHVH as their true God, otherwise they would not be redeemed. So, only 'New Songs' addressed to YHVH, who sits on the throne, will be heard in His Kingdom.

And a 'new Song' doesn't come out of a book, off a piece of paper, nor is the product of someone else's thinking, feelings or experiences – those are the 'old songs' from a church hymnal. All of the redeemed have a 'new song', because each 'new song' is made up of the redeemed person's own personal thoughts, feelings, and experiences as they joyfully sing a song of praise, worship and thanksgiving, which originates from the hearts of the redeemed. Even if the 'new song' is not song audibly, and it has no musical tune, rhythms or notes, yet, YHVH wants to hear that joyful 'new song' in the hearts of all the redeemed.

## CLOSING ARGUMENTS

John wrote God's revelation as it was given to him through Jesus, like a closing argument in a trial. The evidence for a crime against God is in Chapters 2 and 3 where the seven churches are examined and they are found to be rebellious and unfaithful. And again Chapter 6 where the four horses show apostasy in the Christian Church is leading to spiritual death. Then the solution is given from the problem, in Chapter 14 where the true Gospel is clearly given - and it is eternal and timeless gospel, called the **Everlasting Gospel** – it is the final authority as to what the true gospel message is. And it isn't based on what Jesus did on the cross, it's based on what God has done to, and for mankind and expects in return. It doesn't mention Jesus or the cross, nor does it negate the law of God nor does it offer a free pass to heaven by 'believing' some facts. The everlasting gospel basically the same as what Jesus, the Apostles and the disciples preached in the Gospels. The Everlasting Gospel is how we come out of Babylon the Great and how we become one of the redeemed.

Most Gospels that are presented in our churches today simply tell us why and how we are saved. But according to Roman 10:16, 1Peter 4:17, and 2Thessalonians, the true gospel must have commands to obey.

2 Thessalonians 1:8, "**in flaming fire taking vengeance on those who do not know God, and on those who do not obey the gospel of our Lord Jesus Christ.**"

The Everlasting Gospel is in stark contrast to the Gospel based on Paul's letters that is embraced by today's church. It is called the 'Everlasting Gospel' because it lays out the means of salvation for those in the Old Testament era and also for those in the New Testament era. And it is for Jews and Gentiles alike, forever. The commands enumerated by this Everlasting Gospel are already contained in the Old Testament, so the Jews are familiar with these commands. So, it is placed here primarily for the Gentiles who don't know the Old Testament.

## THE FIRST ANGEL'S MESSAGE - THE EVERLASTING GOSPEL

The Everlasting Gospel is so important, and it is Divine in nature and God wants us to know that it didn't come from the imagination of John, but from YHVH God Himself, as He passed it on to Jesus through YHVH's angels. Revelation 14:6-7, "**Then I saw another angel flying in the midst of heaven, having the <u>everlasting gospel</u> to preach to those who dwell on the earth—**

to every nation, tribe, tongue, and people— 7 saying with a loud voice, "Fear God and give glory to Him, for the hour of His judgment has come; and worship Him who made heaven and earth, the sea and springs of water."** This is a gospel message has commands to obey.

Who is the God we are to 'fear', 'give glory' and 'worship'?  The last command identifies who 'God' is, it says, "**worship Him who made heaven and earth, the sea and springs of water**."  If we go to the Forth Commandments (Exodus 20:11) to see who it was that "**made the heaven and earth, the sea and the springs of water**", we will see that it was YHVH God. So, it's clear that the "God" spoken about in this Everlasting Gospel is YHVH God, also known as 'Our Father' (Isaiah 63:16, 64:8, 2Chronicles 29:10, Malachi 1:6-7).  And it is no coincidence that the redeemed (in verse 14:1) had that same name 'YHVH' written 'on' or literally 'in' their foreheads.  And now we know that this Everlasting Gospel is telling us to fear YHVH God, give glorify to YHVH God and worship YHVH God, and that's how to be one of the 144,000 redeemed.

These three commands are given to '**all nations, tribes, tongue and people**' – the 'Nations' are the Gentiles, (the Jews already practiced these three commands as part of their religion, for they are straight out of the Torah that the Jews embrace) this message was given to the Christians in the Christian church, they are commanded to; to Fear YHVH God, give YHVH God glory, and worship YHVH God – and obeying that Everlasting Gospel will put a person among the redeemed, the symbolic **144,000.**  Unfortunately, most of the Christian Church's doctrines, and the 'gospel' they teach, are contrary to the Everlasting Gospel, as I will explain below.

Embedded within Deuteronomy 13:4 we find the three commands of the Everlasting Gospel, "**You shall walk after YHVH your God and fear Him, - and** *(glorify Him by)* **keep His commandments and obey His voice; you shall serve** *(or worship)* **Him and hold fast to Him.**"  Deuteronomy Chapter 13 is a chapter that condemns idolatry and apostasy.  Worshiping the Trinity is idolatry, and practicing lawlessness is apostasy.

When Jesus was on earth he told us to fear YHVH God (Matthew 21:34), glorify YHVH God (Matthew 5:16) and worship YHVH God (Matthew 4:10). Those are the three components of the Everlasting Gospel.  And Revelation 14:4 tells us that the 144,000 redeemed 'follow the Lamb wherever he goes'. That means they follow his teachings and examples.  So, if we follow the Lamb, as he instructed us in Matthew 4:10, 5:16, and 21:34 we will be obeying the Everlasting Gospel even before we hear it from the first angel's message.

### EVERLASTING GOSPEL COMMAND #1 – FEAR YHVH GOD

What does it mean to FEAR YHVH GOD? The Bible is our best dictionary on the matter – The phrase occurs 29 times in the Bible. Different Bible dictionaries define 'fear' somewhat differently. But in the Bible the phrase 'Fear God' is always linked to those who are righteous and hate evil – with the consideration that Judgment is coming. In other words those that 'fear God' keep His commandments and repent when they fail – they are blameless and upright and shun evil. Deuteronomy 13:4, **"You shall walk after YHVH your God and <u>fear Him</u>, and keep His commandments and obey His voice; you shall serve Him and hold fast to Him."** Perhaps "fear" could better be understood as a 'fearful respect' as we fearfully respect fire, poisonous snakes, and bare electric wires. Those who are evil and lawless have no 'fear of God' (See Genesis 22:12, Job 1:1, Ecclesiastes 12:13, Acts 10:2) – for they don't consider the coming Judgment. Those who don't fear God are the fools who don't believe in Him (Psalm 14) or they are convinced that the law is done away with so there will be no judgment for practicing lawlessness, i.e., spurning YHVH's Divine Authority.

The wicked should fear God in terror because of God's judgment is coming. The righteous should have a healthy fear that they may displease the God whom they love and respect. All who properly 'fear God' will obey Him and repent of their sins, and they will then be among the redeemed. Isaiah 59:20, **"The Redeemer will come to Zion, to those in Jacob who repent of their sins," declares YHVH.**" The 'fear of God' drives people to repentance so they will be redeemed and accepted as one of His saint. True repentance is turning from being a violator of God's law to being a keeper of God's law.

Unfortunately not all people fear God because our modern churches tells people that they don't need to keep the law of God, or even the Ten Commandments, and they convince people that they won't be judged for their lawlessness so why fear God. The Sabbath commandment is broken by nearly all Christians that have listened to the great harlot tell them to keep Sunday instead. Some keep the Sabbath but they break the more important First Commandment when they fail to worship YHVH God alone as both Jesus and YHVH commanded. The great harlot convinced them that God is a Trinity. And most all Christian reject God's Passover and eat their Easter Sunday Ham dinners instead – which is an abomination to YHVH God. But, they figure, if we are not under the law and God won't judge us for violating it, why fear God.

Rejecting the need to keep YHVH's 'law and the Prophets' is casted in the concrete of a Christian Church doctrine, so there is no hope for correction. Since the Christian Church can't be corrected, God calls us to get out of it.

**EVERLASTING GOSPEL COMMAND #2 – GIVE YHVH GOD GLORY**

What does it mean to "**give God glory**"?  We cannot make God glorious, He already is.  But we can acknowledge His glory (His goodness, holiness, mercy, love, compassion, wisdom) as we thank and praise Him in new songs, prayer, word and deed.  Psalm 30:12, **"To the end that my glory may sing praise to You and not be silent. O YHVH my God, I will give thanks to You forever."**  We also praise and thank Him for miracles and the marvelous deeds He has performed, especially for creation, sustaining life, His revealed word, healing, forgiveness, and the hope we have.  We are also to glorify His name, YHVH.  We glorify God when we honor Him enough to obey Him.  That's what it means to '**Give Glory to Him**'.  And if we don't honor, fear, and give glory to our future king, we will not be welcomed into His future kingdom.

We take God's glory away when we credit creation to evolution, a natural process, or to Jesus.  We take glory away from God when we give Jesus credit for redemption, instead of the Father who orchestrated it by sending His son to teach us the way?  Aren't we failing to give God glory when we go to Jesus for forgiveness instead of the Father?  Aren't we failing to give God glory when we pray and sing to Jesus and praise Jesus instead of the Father?  Aren't we failing to give God glory when we ignore His Divine name, "YHVH", which He told us to glorify?

Most of the songs and hymns in the Christian Church's hymnals glorifies Jesus and praises Jesus while Our Father is ignored. And worshiping the Trinity (Father, Son, and Holy Spirit) does not worship YHVH Our Father. YHVH will not be worshiped with other gods, for He said we are to worship Him alone and there are no other gods.  To worship the Trinity actually dishonors YHVH, for it violates His direct commandments, such as Exodus 20:2-3, **"I am YHVH your God, who brought you out of the land of Egypt, out of the house of bondage, you shall have no other gods before Me."** And worshiping the Trinity violates Jesus direct command, for he told us to worship and serve YHVH alone (Matthew 4:10).

Worshiping the Trinity is cast in the concrete of a Christian Church doctrine, so there is no hope for correction.  Since the Christian Church can't be corrected, God calls us out of it.

Obey the Everlasting Gospel and give glory to God.  The wicked will not glorify God (See Psalm 86:12, Isaiah 24:15, Luke 2:20, Luke 17:18, Luke 5:25, Luke 18:43, 1 Corinthians 6:20, Romans 15:9, 1 Peter 4:16).

Revelation 15:4, **"Who shall not fear You, YHVH, and glorify Your name?"** More than forty times in the Scriptures we are called on to 'glorify His name'.  We are commanded to glorify the name of YHVH.  How many in the Christian Church even know the God's name is YaHoVeH or "YHVH", and then praise, or glorify His name, as He commands us.  That name is not used, or taught in the Christian Churches, they hide it.  The Christian Church fails here miserably because they are so focused on Jesus that they are rejecting YHVH God Our Father.

### EVERLASTING GOSPEL COMMAND #3 – WORSHIP YHVH

Who are we to worship? Jesus told us to <u>worship YHVH God alone (Matthew 4:10)</u> and YHVH God told us to worship Him alone (Exodus 20:2-3), but the Christian Church tells us to worship the Trinity.

Like the Book of the Revelation, the Book of Zechariah is an apocalyptic book, telling of end time events and judgments. We read of a Judgment scene in Zechariah 13:8-9, **"And it shall come to pass in all the land,"** Says YHVH, **"That two-thirds in it shall be cut off and die, But one-third shall be left in it: I will bring the one-third through the fire, Will refine them as silver is refined, And test them as gold is tested. They will call on My name, And I *(YHVH)* will answer them. I will say, 'This is My people'; And each one will say, 'YHVH is my God.' "**

In this Chapter of Zechariah we find God judgment on idolatry. In these verses YHVH God determines: who are His people, who worship Him, and who do not. YHVH God will do that by subjecting all the people still alive to the 'refining fire' of pain, sorrow, suffering, anguish, fear, and hunger as produced by the plagues of Revelation. In their anguish, all who believe in a god will cry out to their god for deliverance from their dire situation. Those who belong to YHVH God will cry out to Him for deliverance, and He will say to the angels who are inflicting judgments, 'these are my people'. And He will deliver them from their anguish. As we read in the Book of Joel; Joel 2:32, **"And it shall come to pass that whoever calls on the name of the YHVH shall be saved."**

However, those who cried out to Jesus, the Trinity, Mary, or some other god will not be delivered, but will receive all the plagues and judgments in full force. They will **"drink of the wine of the wrath of God, which is poured out full strength into the cup of His indignation"** (Revelation 14:10).

YHVH God will save those who are His from the final judgment.

YHVH must be our only god, the sole object of our worship, and our primary means of worship is by obedience to His will. Submitting to YHVH's Divine authority, as our highest authority is the greatest act of worship we can offer Him. And rejecting His authority is the greatest dishonor we can do to Him. We can't not worship YHVH God and reject His laws.

Unfortunately the Christian Church tells us that we don't need to keep God's commands and laws, which are an expression of His Divine authority. So the Christian Church is telling us that we don't need to submit to YHVH's Divine authority. And if we rejecting YHVH as our greatest authority, that means we have allowed some other authority to become our greatest authority, whom we accept as a greater authority than YHVH God!

YHVH's First Commandment written by His own finger in a tablet of stone states, **"I am YHVH your God, who brought you out of the land of Egypt, out of the house of bondage, you shall have no other gods before Me"** (Exodus 20:2-3). This is not just the first, but it is the most important of all commandments, Jesus said it was the head, or chief, commandment. If we violate this commandment, if we get it wrong, it doesn't matter whether or not we keep any of the other commandments, because we will be worshiping and serving the wrong god. Revelation 14:1 said that the 'redeemed' had the Father's Name (Yahoveh, or YHVH) written in their foreheads–because they are His and that is whom they love, serve and worshiped.

## WHAT IS WORSHIP?

What is worship? The word 'worship' appears 197 times in the Bible. What does the Bible mean by 'worship'? The word comes for the conjunction of two words 'worth' and 'ship'. It means to attribute worth to something – the greatest worth. The act of worship in the Bible has to do with bowing down or prostrate yourself before whoever or whatever it is you are willing to sacrifice for, or submit to. It's not so much the physical position you're in that constitutes an act of worship, but rather it is the attitude of the will, heart and mind that constitutes true worship (John 4:23). To bow or prostrate is a sign of humble submission, to totally submit ourselves to another is an act of worship. To totally submit to God's laws and commands is to obey them, and that is an act of worship. When we obey YHVH God out of love and reverence we are worshiping YHVH God. When we refuse to obey, even though we may physically bow and prostrate our self, pray and sing songs to Him, it is not true worship, it is then as Jesus said, '**you are worshiping in vain**'.

## TRUE WORSHIP

True worship isn't just submission, because we submit to many authorities; parents, teachers, leaders of all types, police, spouse, doctors, bosses, IRS, God, Jesus, etc. Worship is total submission to an authority which we consider to be our greatest authority, or our supreme authority. We will obey our greatest, or supreme, authority above all other authorities, should there ever be a conflict in their commands. Peter and the other Apostles knew that YHVH God was to be their greatest authority, even above the authority of the high priest and the council. Peter said, **"But Peter and the other apostles answered and said: "We ought to obey God rather than men."** I'm sure that Peter and the other apostles normally obeyed the high priest and the council, except when their command conflicted with God's command, then they obeyed

God's command and spurned the authority of the high priest and the council. YHVH God was their greatest authority.

And in Exodus 1:15-17 we read about the midwives Shiparah and Puah who set aside the orders of the king of Egypt, the Pharaoh, and obeyed God because they 'feared God' more that they feared Pharaoh. YHVH God was their greater authority, so they obeyed YHVH God over any other authority. Christians need this same thought and attitude. They need to obey YHVH God's words spoken by Jesus, instead of Church doctrines, the words of their priest, pastor, or whoever. Jesus spoke YHVH's words with His authority.

We can only worship our greatest authority, because any other authorities' commands we will be disobeyed when there is a conflict with the commands of our greatest authority. And we cannot worship an authority that we are willing to dishonor with disobedience – which means we can only worship whoever it is that we accept as our greatest authority, or supreme authority.

Because the Pharisees set aside a commandment of God to keep their traditions, the Pharisees were told that they have an authority greater than YHVH God, so YHVH God was not their greatest authority and therefore their worship of YHVH God was in vain (Mark 7:7-8). When we lay aside even one of YHVH God's laws, or commands, it means that we have an authority greater than YHVH God, and that authority gave us permission to set aside YHVH God's law(s) or command(s).

If YHVH God is not our greatest authority, our greatest authority is usually 'self'. And that happens when the Church convinces us that we are not under God's laws so we don't have to keep them. Then 'self' decides what is 'right and wrong' and what laws to keep and which laws to discard. And even though 'self' becomes our supreme authority, we may still keep some, or most of God's commandments, but He is not our true god, because He is not our supreme authority. Our supreme authority, whomever we choose as our greatest authority, is our true god.

But Bible clearly tells us to worship and serve YHVH alone, giving Him the highest authority, honor and respect, and having no other gods. The Trinity doctrine says there are three co-equal gods that all get the highest authority, honor and respect. YHVH will not be part of such a scheme, for He said He would not share His glory or worship with another god. Perhaps the best and most tangible way we can worship YHVH God is to study His word, and totally submit ourselves to that Word in obedience. That's what it means to worship YHVH God.

The Christian church today worships the 'Trinity', instead of YHVH – stealing glory, honor and worship from YHVH God. The 'church' is telling people that they are saved by their mental faith, what they believe in their hearts, so they don't have keep the commandments of God, and therefore they need not fear God. And true worship is impossible without obedience, that is worshiping in vain. And the 'church' is giving all glory to Jesus, ignoring the Father, in violation of the Everlasting Gospel.

## TWO REASONS TO OBEY THE EVERLASTING GOSPEL;

### EVERLASTING GOSPEL REASON #1 – THE JUDGMENT

The Angel gives us two reasons why we must obey the Everlasting Gospel. The first reason is that Judgment is coming and there will soon be eternal punishment given to those that don't obey the Everlasting Gospel, and eternal rewards will be given to those who obey the Everlasting Gospel, so we need to get right with YHVH God before that time. Fear YHVH God, glorify YHVH God, worship YHVH God alone, and we must repent when we sin.

"Judgment is coming" even the deceived are looking forward to God's judgment because they are deceived into believing that they are right with God – while they are lost and condemned sinners. This will be a most sad time for the deceived, and the Christian Church is full of deceived people. Those who are wicked and lawless, who are still alive, and know they are in violation of God's will, have an opportunity to repent before the final judgment. As both John the Baptizer and Jesus preached, "**Repent for the Kingdom of God is at hand**". The final judgment is good news for God's people. Along with judgment of the wicked comes the end of lawlessness and persecutions of the righteous, and paradise for the faithful.

Matthew 13:41-43, (NASB) **"The Son of Man will send forth His angels, and they will gather out of His kingdom all stumbling blocks, and those who commit lawlessness, and will throw them into the furnace of fire; in that place there will be weeping and gnashing of teeth. Then the righteous will shine forth as the sun in the kingdom of their Father. He who has ears, let him hear."** This is why we must 'fear YHVH God' and be diligent to keep His commandments and laws, lest we become one of those who 'practice lawlessness'. Repent for the Kingdom of God is at hand.

### EVERLASTING GOSPEL REASON #2 – HE IS OUR CREATOR

The Angels give us yet another reason to obey the Everlasting Gospel, YHVH God made us, so we are His. If He is our Maker, we are His property and under His Divine authority. Only a deceived person, or a rebel without fear of God, would dare reject His Divine authority and disobey their Creator, their God, Master, Lawgiver, Judge and King. We must fear Him, glorify Him, obey Him and worship Him. He created us, we are His and if we aren't faithful to

Him He has every right to destroy us, and the potter has the right to destroy flawed pots.

## **NOT FOR CHRISTIANS**

Christians cannot and will not keep the Everlasting Gospel, they can't. To be a Christian one must worship the Trinity and accept it as their god, which is in violation of the YHVH's First Commandment. Christians violate the Second Commandment when they make the 'man Jesus' (Acts 2:22) into a God. Christian generally violate the Third Commandment by claiming to be God's people, called by His name, but then they reject His commands and live lawlessly. And Christians generally worship on Sunday, violation of the Forth Commandment. Christians are told that they don't need to keep YHVH's laws, but they to just believe in Jesus. Christians don't fear YHVH God, glorify YHVH God and they don't worship YHVH God. (We cannot reject or ignore any of YHVH's laws or Commandments, and still worship Him, that worship would be in vain, as it was for the Pharisees in Mark 7:7-9. That why YHVH God call Christians to 'come out of her'.

However, should a Christian start obeying the commands of the Everlasting Gospel, they will cease to be Christian and then become one of the 144,000 Redeemed.

## **A COUNTERFEIT GOSPEL?**

We read the Everlasting Gospel in Revelation 14:6-7, "**Then I saw another angel flying in the midst of heaven, having the everlasting gospel to preach to those who dwell on the earth—to every nation, tribe, tongue, and people— 7 saying with a loud voice, "Fear God and give glory to Him, for the hour of His judgment has come; and worship Him who made heaven and earth, the sea and springs of water**." Three commands were not given here to the Jews, but to '**all nations, tribes, tongue and people**'; to Fear God, give Him glory, and worship YHVH. The Jews knew from their Torah, for centuries, that they were to practice these things, it was the Gentiles who were ignorant of the ways of God and needed to be told.

In Revelation 16:13 we see a corrupted Gospel message, "**And I saw three unclean spirits like frogs *coming* out of the mouth of the dragon, out of the mouth of the beast, and out of the mouth of the false prophet.**" John could have written; "**And I saw out of the three unclean *'teachings'* from the mouth of the dragon, the beast and the false prophet.**" All three, the 'dragon (Satan), the beast (Christian Church) and the false Prophet (Paul), each had all three unclean teachings.

This, I believe, is the corruption of the Everlasting Gospel message. *(The dragon, the beast, and the false prophet each give a message, these three false teachings are negating the three commands of the Everlasting Gospel just as they are negated in our churches today: 1. The Everlasting Gospels commands us to* **'fear YHVH God'** *but one of the false messages in our churches to day says that 'you need not fear God and keep His commandments' for you are saved by what you think. (The Church doctrine that we are not under the law because we are saved by grace apart from obedience to God's law, so there is no need to fear God.) 2. The Everlasting Gospel tells us to* **'give YHVH God glory'** *but this false message is in our churches today is that 'you need not glorify God with your lifestyle', and the church doctrine of redemption gives all credit and glory to Jesus, ignoring the Father 'who so loved us that He sent His son'. 3. The Everlasting Gospel tells us to* **worship YHVH God** *who made the heavens and the earth, but the false gospel (church doctrine of the Trinity) tells 'us to worship the Trinity and gives Jesus credit for Creation and Redemption).* The contemporary Christian church doctrines today that tells us to 'worship the Trinity, primarily Jesus, we are to give him all glory for he freed us from the law and took away our sins, and we need not live holy lives to be saved, but 'just believe in your heart' and you will be saved. And that's all exactly the opposite of the 'Everlasting Gospel'.

## **WHAT IS THE GOSPEL IN TODAY'S CHRISTIAN CHURCHES?**

I viewed a number of WEB sites, looking for an orthodox Christian definition of their 'gospel' is. The Gospels I found were based on Paul's theology, i.e., it is Pauline. I selected four that are representative of what I found;

Gospel #1 from Wikipedia - "Jesus, who is God in flesh (Col. 2:9), bore our sins in His body on the cross (1 Pet. 2:24). He died in our place. He paid the penalty of breaking the Law of God that should have fallen upon us. He satisfied the law of God the Father by dying on the cross."

Gospel #2 from Billy Graham- What is the Gospel? Let us ask Paul for the answer. He wrote: "Now, brothers, I want to remind you of the gospel I preached to you, which you received and on which you have taken your stand. By this gospel you are saved ... For what I received I passed on to you as of first importance: that Christ died for our sins according to the Scriptures, that he was buried, that he was raised on the third day according to the Scriptures, and that he appeared to Peter, and then to the Twelve" (1 Corinthians 15:1-5, NIV)."

Gospel #3 from the ELCA Lutherans; "The message of the gospel is the good news that a loving God sent Jesus Christ to take away the sins of all people. This gospel freely offers to all sinners the righteousness that is found in Jesus. God offers and gives eternal life and salvation to all those who believe in the gospel promises."

Gospel #4 from a Baptist Church; 1. Jesus, God's only son, died to pay the price for your sin. *Romans 5:8 But God commendeth his love toward us, in that, while we were yet sinners, Christ died for us.*

2. You can be saved from your sin today. *Romans 10:13 For whosoever shall call upon the name of the Lord shall be saved.*

3. Pray and ask Jesus Christ to be your Savior, and claim His promise of eternal life.

*Dear Lord, I know that I am a sinner. I know that Jesus died on the cross for me. I repent of my sin, please forgive me and save me. In Jesus' name, Amen.*

While worded a little different, they are very similar. But they are all in sharp contrast to God's Everlasting Gospel. These gospels simply tell us that as a sinner we are saved by Jesus who died for our sins and all we have to do is to believe it, claim it, or 'call on the name of Jesus. These gospels are in complete contrast to the Everlasting Gospel where there are calls to fear YHVH God, glorify YHVH God and worship YHVH God, that will produce personal righteousness, repentance, and obedience by keeping God's commandments.

But you ask, 'must we keep all of God's laws?' According to Paul the answer is 'no', but according to Jesus the answer is 'yes'. How do we deal with that? First of all, who is the greater authority? Jesus, of course. And Jesus said if we keep his word we will never see death.

While Paul did say that we have died to the law (Romans 7:6, Galatians 2:19), we are not under the law (Romans 6:14) and all things are lawful for believers (1Corithinas 6:12), he also had verses that said that the law is holy, just and good (Romans 7:12), and it is most important that we keep God's law (1Corinthians 7:19). He also wrote a number of times that law breakers will not inherit the kingdom of God (1Corinthians 6:9-11). And in Acts 24:14 he confessed his Jewish faith in one God and the 'law and the prophets'. How do we reconcile these with his seemingly contradictory verses in Paul's epistles?

We also have to remember that Paul was a Pharisee and Jesus said the Pharisees were 'lawless hypocrites' (Matthew 23:28), and indeed Paul was often accused of lying, and he defended himself a number of times by claimed, "I'm not lying" (Romans 9:1, 2Corthians 11:31, 1Timothy 3:7). Then in 1st Corinthians 9:19-23 he admitted that he lied to deceive others. And, Jesus said the he himself is to be our only teacher, so we can set Paul confusing words aside and listen to and follow Jesus instead. Jesus was YHVH anointed Prophets (Deuteronomy 18:18-19, Acts 3:22, 7:37, John 12:49, 14:10) who spoke YHVH's words with YHVH's authority.

So let's go to the Book of the Revelation to see what it says about whether or not we need to keep God's laws.

Three Angels' Messages for the Christian Church

In the Book of Revelation Jesus said that the saints (redeemed) are those that keep the commandments of God. All who are not redeemed are condemned because they practiced lawlessness. Revelation 14:12 (NKJV), **"Here is the patience of the saints; here are those who keep the commandments of God and the faith of Jesus".**

Revelation 12:17 (NKJV), **"And the dragon was enraged with the woman, and he went to make war with the rest of her offspring, who keep the commandments of God and have the testimony of Jesus Christ"**. Satan hates those who keep the commandments of God – because they wouldn't fall for his deceptions and they submit to YHVH's Divine authority. Those that don't keep the commandments are already victims of his deceptions and are in Satan's camp whether they know it or not, they submitting to his authority. Keeping the Testimony of Jesus is simply keeping Jesus' words, which tells us that YHVH God is one, we are to keep the commandments of YHVH God, and worship YHVH alone. 'The Commandments' means all God has commanded – not just the Ten Commandments.

## THE SECOND ANGEL'S MESSAGE – A WARNING

Revelation 14:8 NKJV, **"And another angel followed, saying, "Babylon is fallen, is fallen, that great city, because she has made all nations drink of the wine of the wrath of her fornication."** This is Revelation's first reference to **"Babylon".** Who is Babylon? I know that different Christian denominations like to point to other Christian denominations and say they are Babylon the Great – most Protestant Churches will point to the Roman Catholic Church. The truth is, the entire Christian Church is Babylon. Why is the Christian Church referred to as Babylon? The original trinity worship began in Ancient Babylon with Nimrod – Tammuz – and Semiramis. These three are in the Old Testament, in the Canaanite language, identified as Baal, Ashtoreth, and Tammuz. Nearly all false religions have adopted some form of the trinity, with different names. In AD 325 the Roman Emperor Constantine led the council of Nicea to declare God to be a Trinity. To enforce the decision of the Council of Nicea, Constantine commanded the death penalty for those who would not accept the doctrine of the Trinity. Thus Christianity had adopted the pagan 'Babylonian' Trinity, but now with "Christian" names. That's when the Christian Church became Babylon the Great, and had fallen from God's grace.

We see that same phrase 'Babylon has fallen in Book of Isaiah. Isaiah 21:9, **"And look, here comes a chariot of men with a pair of horsemen!" Then he answered and said, "Babylon is fallen, is fallen! And all the carved images of her gods He has broken to the ground."** The evilness of Babylon was a result of her 'carved images and her gods' – violating the First and Second Commandments – as the Christian Church does. Babylon may have been corrupt and evil in many other ways, but Isaiah's words, as inspired by

YHVH God, pointing to her false gods and false worship. This was written as a warning to God's people that they don't chase after false gods, like the Trinity, and worship of Jesus instead of worship YHVH alone.

God ultimately destroyed the ancient Babylon because of her wickedness in making the nations endure its wrath. And God will bring down the spiritual Babylon. Verse 14:8 is a warning for those in Babylon and essentially a call to get out of the spiritual Babylon (Christian Church), for it has spiritually fallen and will physically fall. How do we get out of Babylon? We get out of spiritual Babylon by keeping the Everlasting Gospel; we are to fear YHVH God alone, glorify YHVH God alone and worship YHVH God alone. Those three commands are not compatible with Christian theology.

And in keeping the Everlasting Gospel, we will have separated ourselves from the Babylonian Christian Church which preaches and teaches contrary to the Everlasting Gospel. The Babylonian Church teaches contrary to God's commands, Jesus' commands and it practices idolatry by worshiping the Trinity.

### THE THIRD ANGEL'S MESSAGE – DON'T WORSHIP THE BEAST

Revelation 14:9-12 (NIKJV), **"Then a third angel followed them, saying with a loud voice, "If anyone worships the beast and his image, and receives his mark on his forehead or on his hand, 10 he himself shall also drink of the wine of the wrath of God, which is poured out full strength into the cup of His indignation. He shall be tormented with fire and brimstone in the presence of the holy angels and in the presence of the Lamb. 11 And the smoke of their torment ascends forever and ever; and they have no rest day or night, who worship the beast and his image, and whoever receives the mark of his name."**

For the Christian, there are only two objects of worship either we worship YHVH God, or we worship the beast (and his image). Who do we worship? We worship whoever is our greatest authority. Who is our greatest authority? YHVH tells us to keep His Commandment, the Beast (Church) tells us that we don't need to, so who are you going to obey? Whoever you choose to obey is your greatest authority, that is your god, and that is who you worship. If we set YHVH's commands aside and obey the beast (church) we are worshiping the beast, by our obedience to him.

In Matthew 13:41-42 we read that those who **"practiced lawlessness"** will, at the end of time, be gathered and cast into the fiery furnace. Now we read in Revelation 14 about those who **'worshiped the beast and his image'** being cast into the same fiery furnace. Is **'practicing lawlessness'** the same as **'worshiping the beast'**? Yes, it is.

If we will not submit to YHVH's Divine authority, by obeying His commands, we are practicing lawlessness. If we are practicing lawlessness it is because we are submitting to the authority of the beast (i.e., the church), who tells us that we don't need to keep God's law and commandments. When we have rejected YHVH's commands, to obey the beast (or his image), then the beast is our greatest authority and obedience to him is an act of worship.

So, submitting to YHVH by obeying His commands (the law and the Prophets) is an act of worship. And, submitting to the beast (or his image) by obeying his teachings to rejecting YHVH's law and the Prophets, is worshipping the beast (or his image). Who is it that tells us we don't need to keep YHVH's 'law and the Prophets'? The 'Church' i.e., the beast, or his image.

A person may be in good standing within the Christian religion, going to church every Sunday to worship God, weekly going to confession, receiving the sacraments and obey all church rules. Yet, if they reject, set aside, or ignore one or more of YHVH's laws they are practicing lawlessness, and they are unknowingly and unwittingly worship the beast by their obedience to him.

Worshiping the beast (or his image) doesn't mean to bow down before a beastly being, or statue, praying, singing, light candles or chanting to a beastly being. We worship the beast by submitting to the beast's (Christian Church's) authority, when it tells us that we don't need to keep YHVH's law and the Prophets and that we are to worship a trinity of gods instead of YHVH.

Christians don't know that they are worshiping the Beast (the Catholic Church) or his image (the Protestant Church). They go to church and do as their church tells them, but in doing that they are placing the Church's authority above YHVH's authority, and thus they are unintentionally worship the Beast, or the image of the Beast –by their submitting to his authority. According to Revelation 14:9, we are either worshiping YHVH God, or the Beast and his image.

Disobedience to YHVH first happened in the Garden of Eden and it was due to the teachings of the 'serpent beast'. Embracing the serpent beast's message, the beast (Church) tells us that we can reject YHVH's Divine authority and there will be no eternal consequences. YHVH God tells us to keep His commandments, the beast (and his image) tells us that we don't have to. Who are you going to believe?

Revelation 14:12, **"Here is the perseverance** (*or patience or endurance*) **of the saints; here are those who keep the commandments of God and the faith of Jesus."** Here, God answers that question and tells us who to believe.

God's saints are those who preserve in keeping the commandments of God and have the faith of Jesus. Two expectations: keep the Commandment and have the faith of Jesus. Keeping the Commandments is to submit to YHVH's Divine authority. Having the 'faith of Jesus' is to believe, and accept the Old Testament as Jesus did.

Those who submit to YHVH's Divine authority will be the redeemed saints of God. Revelation 14:9-12 shows us a contrast between two groups of people; there are those who have the 'Mark of the Beast' (Vs. 9) because they have been defiled by the 'women' and in contrast to that group are those who 'keep the commandments of God' (Vs. 12), they have 'YHVH' written on (in) their foreheads and follow the teachings of the Lamb. So clearly it's those who don't keep the commandments of God who have the Mark of the Beast and will be cast into the fire (Vs. 10-11). And that agrees with Matthew 13:41-42 where Jesus tells us that it's those who 'practice lawlessness' will be gathered at judgment time and cast into a furnace of fire.

To 'practice lawlessness' means that they have rejected, set aside or continually ignored some, or all, of God's laws with no guilt, remorse or thought of repentance. Those with the Mark of the Beast are those who 'practiced lawlessness' we know that because they both end up in that lake of fire – because they are the same group of people.

The 'saints' were able to avoid the lake of fire because they 'persevered' in keeping the Commandments of God and continued to practice the 'faith of Jesus' (Vs. 12) i.e., followed the Lamb. And according to Jesus, in Revelation 22:14, he tells us that it's those who keep the commandments of God who will enter the New Jerusalem by the gates and to eat from the Tree of Life.

Revelation 22:14 mentions that those who do the commandments of God will enter the New Jerusalem "by the gates". "By the gates" is an important but often overlooked phrase. In ancient cities it was at the gates, where the elders sat, and judgment took place. And those who were found to be innocent were allowed into the city (New Jerusalem). And those who were found to be guilty were taken outside the city where they received their just punishment, and in this case, after the final judgment, death by fire and brimstone. What is the criteria for that future final judgment? Jesus tells us in John 5:28-30, where he says that he will judge us according to our deeds, good and bad. And the standard (or law) by which we will be judged is not some New Testament standard, we will be judged according to the will of God, God's Old Testament Law. And in Matthew 7:22-23 we read that those who didn't do the will of God were referred to as those who 'practiced lawlessness', and in Matthew 13:41-42 those who 'practice lawlessness' were gathered and cast into a furnace of fire. (Note; The word 'commandment' in the Scriptures in not specifically referring to the Ten Commandments, but it refers to whatever God has commanded.)

So clearly, God will save those who love Him and keep His commandments, and those who will not keep His commandments will receive the Mark of the Beast, and they will be cast into a furnace of fire – because they have dishonored YHVH by spurning His Divine authority. And I know this is contrary to what Paul said, but it's what Jesus said and it's Jesus who we must listen to. Jesus spoke the words of YHVH God and he will judge us, so we had better not ignore him. In Deuteronomy 18:18-19, YHVH God said He would send His special anointed Prophet to speak His words with His authority, and we had better listen to him, or we will suffer the consequences. The Apostle Peter (Acts 3:22-23) and the first martyr Stephen (Acts 7:37) both testified that Jesus is the Prophet (Christ or Messiah) of Deuteronomy 18:18-19. Then Jesus himself said that he spoke YHVH's words with YHVH's authority (John 14:10, 24), so we better listen to him.

## NO PERFECT OBEDIENCE FOR THE REDEEMED SAINTS

The Scriptures never imply that we must keep the law perfectly, and since we are imperfect beings we can't do that. But it should be our desire and goal to do God's will – which according to Matthew 7:22-23 is God's law. "**Blessed are those who hunger and thirst for righteousness, for they shall be filled**", (Matthew 5:6). To hunger and thirst means that we will not fully be satisfied with our own righteousness, but we strongly desire for it.

When we do sin, and we all do, repentance is required, and true repentance will cover (atone) our sins, so we can be justified (Luke 18:14), made white as snow (Isaiah 1:18) and have our sins blotted out (Acts 3:19). It's not perfect obedience that saves us, for there is no one perfect, but yet we must be willing to submit to all of which YHVH God has commanded. Those who reject God's laws, ignoring them or just won't keep them, are condemned for practicing lawlessness (Matthew 13:41-42). Our desire, effort and willingness to keep God's law is showing God our love and respect for Him as we willingly submit to His Divine authority, and that honors Him as an act of worship. To reject God's commandments, ignoring them, or intentionally setting them aside for any reason, will result in us disobeying God, and that dishonors Him, showing a lack of love, lack of faith/trust, and lack of respect by spurning His Divine authority.

## ARE YOU PREFECT?

So perfection may be needed for salvation, but our perfection doesn't come from us perfectly obeying God's entire law for our entire lives. Our perfection doesn't come from wearing Jesus' robe of righteousness as some people suggest. Our perfection comes to us from YHVH God when we repent of our sins, acknowledge our sin, being sorry for committing them, and having turned away from sin by choosing to keep YHVH's laws which we had violated.

The net result of true repentance is that we have re-committing ourselves to enthrone God as our Supreme Authority and dethroning 'self', the beast, his image anyone else who has usurped YHVH's Divine authority. In doing that, we are made perfect and justified in God's eyes and fit for the Kingdom of heaven.

However, repentance can't happen if we don't accept God's law as binding and having authority over us. Because if we think we are not under the law, and feel no need to keep God's laws, we will never consider ourselves to be sinners and never feel a need to repent, like the Pharisee in the Parable of the Pharisee and the Publican (Luke 18). Jesus said the Publican when home justified, but Jesus never said such a thing about the Pharisee. Being justified is being made as if we have never sinned, perfect in God's eyes.

So when the Christian church, convinces people that they are not under God's Torah law, and they don't need to keep God's law, they deceived people. These deceived people will never attempt to keep God's law, never feel the conviction of sin and then never repent – they will be those who 'practice lawlessness'. Then like the Pharisee, they will die in their sins, being lost and condemned as one who practices lawlessness – receiving the mark of the Beast. Jesus said the Pharisees were lawless (Matthew 23:28) and that is because they set aside a number of God's commandments to keep their man-made traditions (Matthew 15:3, Mark 7:9).

God's word is the Old Testament, Torah and the Prophets, or the 'law and the Prophets' which Jesus told us to keep forever, every jot and tittle. Yet, the Orthodox Jews (today's Pharisees) exalt the Talmud above the 'law and the Prophets' so they will set aside God's law when necessary to keep their Talmud. Muslims do the same with their Koran, and Christians do the same with church doctrines based on Paul's Epistles. In all three cases the authority of the 'law and the Prophets' is superseded by some manmade religious writing.

## **TWO TYPES OF CHRISTIANS**

Ultimately there are two types of Christians. There are the many "doctrinal Christians" who considers themselves Christian because they follow Christian Church doctrines, they do as their pastors or priests tell them, and they attend church on Sundays, or some even on Saturdays. They will set aside Jesus' instructions and God's commands to follow all church's rules, laws, creeds, doctrines, etc. They worship the Trinity and are true Christians according to the Christian Church.

And then there are those who follow and obey Jesus' teachings and instructions, even when they are contrary Christian Church doctrines. They will set aside church doctrine, creeds and teachings when they are contrary to Jesus' words. These are heretics according to the Christian Church. They obey Jesus in keeping YHVH's law and the Prophets and they worship YHVH alone. So, who are the true Christians, those who follow Church teachings or those who follow Jesus' teachings?

And again, Jesus isn't suggesting that we are saved by our mechanical keeping of His commandments and the law. But, only those who 'follow the Lamb', keep, desire to keep, or attempt to keep, God's commands, and that demonstrates their love for God, their faith in God, the fearful respect of God, and their willingness to submit to YHVH's Divine authority. Those who simply adhere to Christian Church doctrines believe contrary to what Jesus instructed as how to enter the kingdom of God.

## **WHAT IS THE MAIN MESSAGE IN THE BOOK OF THE REVELATION?**

The bottom line of the Book of the Revelation is Chapter 14, and the middle of Chapter 14 is the Three Angels' messages. God doesn't just call us out of Babylon, but in Chapter 14 we learn why we must leave, and He tells us what we must do to get out of the corrupt Babylonian Church.

We are called to fear YHVH God, glorify YHVH God and worship YHVH God and that means we must submit to His Divine authority. So, don't let anyone, or any of Paul's writing, any church creed or doctrine deceive you into setting aside any of God's laws, or rejecting God's authority in favor of the Church's authority, for then we are in danger of judgment. Whoever you obey as your greatest authority and that is your true god, and that is whom you worship through your obedience.

We must worship YHVH alone – and obedience is an important act of worship – without obedience there is no worship, for disobedience is an act of rebellion – the opposite of worship.

Be faithful to the end, we must repent when we fail, and God will welcome us into the New Jerusalem and give us the gift of eternal life.

Few will be saved.... Revelation 12:9-13:3 says, '**all the world is deceived and follow after the beast**', that means a great majority of people are deceived. Matthew 7:13-14, Jesus said only a '**few**' find the narrow gate and travel on the narrow way to eternal life, while the 'many' are on the Broad way to eternal destruction. Jesus said his flock is a small one (Luke 12:23). The word 'small' is the Greek word 'micro'. Revelation refers to the redeemed as the 144,000. While the 144,000 may not be a literal number, it will be a small group who are redeemed – not the billion who call themselves Christians. Why is the group to be redeemed so small? Christians don't qualify if the worship the Trinity or Jesus, and they won't keep YHVH's laws and Prophets. Muslims don't qualify if they accept the authority of their Koran over the authority of God's word. The Jews who accept the 'oral tradition' (Talmud) over the authority of God's word won't qualify, either. Only those who "fear YHVH God, glorify YHVH God and worship YHVH God" will qualify – and that is a small group.

End of Revelation

# CHAPTER 5 – PAUL

## PAUL THE DECEIVER

We can't understand the problems in the Christian Church or the need for the Three Angel's Message until we understand Paul and his theology. Paul's theology was far different from that of Jesus or Jesus' true apostles and yet the church embraces Paul's theology to the exclusion of the teachings of Jesus or his apostles. That's not saying that they completely dismiss all the Jesus said, but when it comes to the way of salvation, Jesus is replaced with Paul. They interpret John 3:16 in a fashion that supports Paul's theology. That means they believe salvation is by having 'faith in Jesus'. However, Jesus and his apostles would say that salvation by having the 'faith of Jesus'. And there is significant difference between having 'faith in Jesus' and having the 'faith of Jesus'.

Paul's theology leads directly to lawlessness, because it is quite easy for a person to be lawless and at the same time have 'faith in Jesus' – our prison system are full of this type of people. And that is not true with those who have the 'faith of Jesus'. The 'faith of Jesus' is that of Biblical Judaism, believing and living the Torah laws, such as Jesus did, and we see very few of these people in the prison system.

And while Paul didn't believe in a Triune God, Paul deified Jesus, making Jesus an object of worship and a great source of idolatry, and Paul's writings were the foundation for the formulation of a Trinity doctrine centuries later.

## WHY ARE PAUL'S TEACHINGS CONTRARY TO JESUS' TEACHINGS?

According to Isaiah 42:21 the Messiah came to exalt the YHVH's law and Jesus did that (Matthew 5:17-19), telling us to keep every jot and tittle, even the least commandment until heaven and earth pass away. And Jesus tells us that those who don't keep his word will not receive eternal life (Matthew 7:24-27, John 8:51) Yet, Paul tells us more than 36 times that we are not under the YHVH's law and we don't need to keep it.

Paul never met Jesus, and he didn't have the Gospels, which were written by Jesus' apostles, to teach him about Jesus, for they weren't written yet. Paul had a vision of a spirit that he believed was Jesus, but that 'spirit's' message was so contrary to what Jesus taught and spoke, it is unlikely that it was Jesus.

I know that everybody loves Paul and his epistles. Paul is truly the founder of today's Christian religion. It was Paul who told us that we are free

Three Angels' Messages for the Christian Church

from the law, he told us the law is dead, the law can't save us, it was done away with at the cross, we are saved apart from the law by grace, etc. The entire Christian Church relies heavily on Paul's writings to create their church doctrines. and they base their gospel messages on Paul's writings rather than Jesus' words.

Paul taught 'lawlessness', that is; teaching that we do not need to keep God's law because, according to Paul, obedience to God's law has nothing to do with our salvation – you may not realize it, but Paul's lawless message originated in the Garden of Eden where Adam and Eve were convinced that they didn't need to keep YHVH's law and they could still have eternal life. It's because of that message that God's holy law is lowly esteemed, mostly ignored and only partially kept by Christians. Our jails and our prisons are full of people who define themselves as Christians who have been taught that it's not necessary to keep God's laws, and they believe they are saved if they 'believe in Jesus' so their moral behavior in inconsequential. At the same time, there are almost no Jews in the prison system, and so we have to ask ourselves; why is that? And answer is obvious. Jews have be taught it is important to keep God's laws,

As we have read the story of Adam and Eve, one can easily conclude that it was the serpent beast's lie that turned Adam and Eve into 'lawless' people, after he got Eve to question YHVH's Divine authority and His truthfulness. The serpent's poisonous venom was his 'lawless' teaching by which he deceived Eve, and convinced her that it wasn't necessary to keep YHVH's command, and promised them that there would be no eternal consequences for spurning YHVH's Divine authority (telling her, "surely you will not die") and that only good would come of it; **"Your eyes will be opened and your will be like God knowing good and evil"**.

Paul and the Serpent beast both tell us that it's not necessary to keep YHVH's Divine authority as expressed in His laws, and we still can receive eternal life. Their reasoning may vary, but the practical application of what they say is the same. We don't need to keep YHVH's law and we will still be saved.

That was the serpent beast's deceiving lie that got Adam and Eve to set aside YHVH's law and eat the forbidden fruit. And now, the same serpent beast's lawless message is preached and taught in the Christian Churches. The Church tells us that we don't need to keep YHVH's "Old Covenant" law and surely we will not die because of it for we are saved by God's grace. They tell us that Jesus died and paid the penalty for our sins: past, present and future. Paul tells us that it's for our benefit that we sin, (Romans 5:20) because then we will be forced to trust God for salvation instead of our law keeping.

And if we spurn YHVH's Divine authority by rejecting His laws, then we will have to decide for ourselves which laws to keep and which ones to reject – therefore we subconsciously become our own gods, assuming the role of God in determining what is good and what is evil. That's exactly what the serpent beast told Eve, and Adam was probably heard it as well. Genesis 3:5, **"For God knows that in the day you eat of it your eyes will be opened, and you will be like God, knowing good and evil"**.

When we spurn YHVH's Divine authority by reject His laws, we have rejected Him as our true God, and that is spiritual fornication i.e., idolatry.

How did that lawless message get into the Christian Church? There can only be one answer to that question, and the clear answer is PAUL.

God used the serpent beast in the Garden to test Adam and Eve, to see whether they would obey Him or listen to the serpent beast and follow the dictates of their own hearts and minds. And now God is using Paul to play the part of the serpent beast, i.e., the tempter, for the New Testament Christian era. The temptation is to test the believers as to whether or not, when it comes right down to it, they will obey YHVH God's words (Jesus also spoke YHVH's words), or will they embrace Paul's lawless message and follow the dictates of their own heart and mind.

Just as the serpent beast provided a test for Adam and Eve in the Garden, so Paul provides the exact same test for us. Paul provides us with a convenient 'New Testament' excuse to spurn YHVH's, and Jesus' authorities. And that's all the excuse most people need, especially those who really don't want to keep YHVH's laws and commandments anyway. Why did Paul tell us that we don't need to keep YHVH's law? Keep reading and you will soon understand Paul's reasoning.

## I COULD HAVE DONE BETTER THAN ADAM AND EVE

As we look back at the Adam and Eve story, I think we can all agree that they did wrong, and we like to think that if we were in the Garden we would have resisted the cunning serpent beast's deception. Right? Well, we're not in the Garden of Eden, but we do have that same opportunity to resist the serpent's deceptive lie today, because we have that same temptation, with the same deceptive message that Adam and Eve had – but this time it's coming from Paul's epistles as they're preached to everyone in the Christian Churches – a place where we would least expect serpent's deceptive message coming from. And that's probably the same caliber of a test as the serpent's message to Adam and Eve in YHVH's paradise Garden, where they would least expect to hear a deceptive message.

Jesus told us to keep the Old Testament 'law and the Prophets', every jot and tittle until heaven and earth passes away. Yet, Paul, said we didn't have to keep YHVH's law and the Prophets, he tells us the law was nailed to the cross, done away with, it was the Old Covenant, it was just given by angels, it was only a temporary tutor, it works wrath, the law causes us to sin and many other reasons why we don't need to keep YHVH's laws. Why the difference between the messages of Jesus and Paul? Keep reading and you will soon understand why there is a difference between their understandings of the way of salvation.

## JESUS SAID WATCH OUT FOR THE TEACHINGS OF THE PHARISEES

Throughout the New Testament Scriptures we read that Jesus continually had confrontations with the Pharisees. Jesus had the harshest words for them, and they even called Jesus a sinner and plotted his death. And that should raise a big red flag for us about the Pharisees' belief, religion and theology. Jesus spoke YHVH's words with YHVH's authority, and so anyone who speaks contrary to what Jesus spoke is also speaking contrary to the words of YHVH our God.

Jesus clearly understood the flaws with the Pharisees' way of thinking and in their teachings, and so Jesus warned his disciples about them. Matthew 16:12 NKJV, **"Then they understood that He did not tell them to beware of the leaven of bread, but of the doctrine of the Pharisees and Sadducees."** And we should accept this as a warning from Jesus about what Paul the Pharisee is teaching us in his epistles. Matthew 23:28, **"Even so you also outwardly appear righteous to men, but inside you are full of hypocrisy and lawlessness".**

What was the problem with the teachings (or doctrines) of the Pharisees that we must beware of? We are told that while they acted very pious, righteous and religious, they were actually "lawless hypocrites". Why did Jesus consider them to be "lawless hypocrites"?

## JESUS SAID THE PHARISEES WERE LAWLESS

Before we discuss why Jesus considered the Pharisees to be lawless we must discuss what the Scriptures mean by 'lawless' or one 'practicing lawlessness'. Only when we understand what 'lawlessness' is can we understand why the Pharisees were considered to be lawless. Jesus said, (John 7:19 (NKJV)), **"Has not Moses given you the law? Yet not one of you keeps the law. Why are you trying to kill me?"**

A 'lawless' person may keep some, or even most of YHVH's laws and appear to be religious, moral and righteous, but in rejecting even one of God's laws, minor as it may seem, that person has spurned YHVH's Divine authority, dishonored Him, despised His word, and committed an act of rebellion – that is lawlessness. That person may seem religious, attend church weekly, receive communion or the sacrament, be an Elder, or even a pastor/priest, but they reject one or more of YHVH's laws. In rejecteing even one minor law and are spurning YHVH's Divine authority and in doing that they are displaying a lack of faith, fear, reverence, respect and love for God. When a person is deceived into believing that they don't need to keep YHVH's laws, they are in fact rejecting, or spurning YHVH's Divine authority – that's how the serpent beast got Eve to sin. After a person sets YHVH's law(s) aside as obsolete, out of date, or somehow no longer relevant, they will then violate that law(s) without giving it a second thought, they will feel no guilt, godly sorrow or remorse, and so they will not even consider it to be a sin, so they can't repent. That's why Adam and Eve, after being confronted by God in the Garden, did not repent. And without repentance there is no forgiveness. That is practicing lawlessness.

We all do lawless acts, and some lawless acts are unintentional sins. Unintentional sins happen when we acknowledge that we need to keep the law, but we are overcome by temptation, temporarily deceived, or stumble in a time of moral weakness, and we violate God's law. However, those who sin unintentional will feel guilt, godly sorrow, they then remorse and they repent. By their true repentance, their sins are forgiven, justified, and they are made white as snow. But those who intentionally reject the authority of YHVH God's laws, will violate those 'obsolete' laws as a presumptuous sinner and will never feel guilt, remorse nor will they repent.

2Corinthians 7:10, "For godly sorrow produces repentance leading to salvation, not to be regretted; but the sorrow of the world *(i.e., without repentant)* produces death".

God expresses His Divine authority by His laws. "Lawlessness" is the rejection of YHVH's Divine authority, even if it is the rejecting just one of His laws, and that, of course, results in the violation of those rejected law(s). They who sin because they have rejected YHVH's laws sin presumptuously without repentance.

A presumptuous sinner is one who 'practices lawlessness', they are also known as 'the lawless', 'the wicked' or 'workers of iniquity'. Presumptuous sinners presume the law is not from them, they presume they don't need to keep it, they presume there will be no consequences for violating it, so they freely violate it and presume it's not a sin and so no repentance is necessary. And that's why Jesus called the Pharisees 'lawless', because they set aside certain laws of God (Mark 7:7-9, Matthew 23:23) in order to keep their religious traditions – and they violated those YHVH's laws presumptuously. Mark 7:7-8, **"And in vain they worship Me, teaching as doctrines the commandments of men.' 8 For laying aside the commandment of God, you hold the tradition of men—the washing of pitchers and cups, and many other such things you do."** Apparently there was a commandment of God which was in contention with their traditions - so they set aside God's commandment to keep their tradition.

Peter also saw the lawless results of people embracing Paul's Epistles, for we read in 2Peter 3:16-17 (ESV), "**as he** *(Paul)* **does in all his letters when he speaks in them of these matters. There are some things in them that are hard to understand, which the ignorant and unstable twist to their own destruction, as they do the other Scriptures. 17 You therefore, beloved, knowing this beforehand, take care that you are not carried away with the error of lawless people and lose your own stability."** Those who embrace Paul's words, at the expense of Jesus' words or YHVH's words, end up believing themselves to be saved while they practice lawlessness.

Paul wrote, (Romans 5:20, ESV): **"Now the law came in to increase the trespass, but where sin increased, grace abounded all the more."** Is Paul actually saying the more we rebel against YHVH's Divine authority, and reject YHVH's laws and commandments and sin, the more saving grace we will receive? The purpose of the law was for us to sin?

YHVH God and Jesus told us to keep YHVH's 'law and the Prophets', every jot and tittle until heaven and earth pass away. Jesus also told us that we if don't keep his word will not see eternal life. Yet, Paul gives us no less than 36 reasons why we don't need to keep YHVH God's laws, and I'm not sure this is a complete list, but it is plenty;

The law is an unbearable yoke. (Acts 15:10)
The law reveals sin but cannot fix it. (Romans 3:20)
If the law worked then faith would be irrelevant. (Romans 4:14)
The law brings wrath upon those who follow it. (Romans 4:15)
The purpose of the law was to increase sin. (Romans 5:20)
Christians are not under the law. (Romans 6:14)
Christians have been delivered from the law. (Romans 7:1-6)
The law is good, perfect and holy but cannot help you be good, perfect or holy. (Romans 7:7-12)
The law which promises life only brings death through sin. (Romans 7:10)
The law makes you sinful beyond measure. (Romans 7:13)
The law is weak. (Romans 8:2-3)
The strength of sin is the law (1 Corinthians 15:56)
The law is a ministry of death. (2 Corinthians 3:7)
The law is a ministry of condemnation. (2 Corinthians 3:9)
The law has no glory at all in comparison with the New Covenant. (2 Corinthians 3:10)
The law is fading away. (2 Corinthians 3:11)
Anywhere the law is preached it produces a mind-hardening and a heart-hardening veil. (2 Corinthians 3:14-15)
The law justifies nobody. (Galatians 2:16)

Christians are dead to the law. (Galatians 2:19)
The law frustrates grace. (Galatians 2:21)
To go back to the law after embracing faith is "stupid". (Gal 3:1)
The law curses all who practice it and fail to do it perfectly. (Gal 3:10)
The law has nothing to do with faith. (Galatians 3:11-12)
The law was a curse that Christ redeemed us from. (Galatians 3:13)
The law functioned in God's purpose as a temporary covenant from Moses was until John the Baptist announced Christ. (Galatians 3:16 & 19)
If the law worked God would have used it to save us. (Galatians 3:21)
The law was our prison. (Galatians 3:23)
The law makes you a slave like Hagar. (Galatians 4:24)
Christ has abolished the law which was a wall of hostility (Eph 2:15)
Paul considered everything the law gained him as "skybalon" which is Greek for "poop". (Philippians 3:4-8)
The law is only good if used in the right context. (1Tim 1:8)
It was made for the unrighteous but not for the righteous. (1Tim 1:9-10)
The law is weak, useless and makes nothing perfect. (Hebrews 7:18-19)
God has found fault with it and created a better covenant, enacted on better promises. (Hebrews 8:7-8)
It is obsolete, growing old and ready to vanish. (Hebrews 8:13)
It is only a shadow of good things to come and will never make someone perfect (Hebrews 10:1).
Our Election is not by the law but by promise (Galatians 3:17-18).
We are saved by confessing and believing - not the law(Romans 10:9-10).

And Paul is correct to say that we are not saved by our mechanical obedience to God's laws. But, what Paul fails to say is that at the same time those who refuse to keep God's laws are spurning His Divine authority and evoking God's wrath. But, God loves those who love Him and keeps His commandments and they alone honor God, fearfully respect God and love God, and they alone will receive His saving grace.

## A SMALL SECT OF THE PHARISEES WERE NOT LAWLESS

Here, below, is an interesting verse; it says some (a sect, or small group) of the Pharisees "believed" and were convinced, that it was necessary to keep the Law of Moses. Acts 15:5 (NKJV), "**But some of the sect of the Pharisees who believed rose up, saying, "It is necessary to circumcise them, and to command them to keep the law of Moses."** So, there were some Pharisees (only a sect) who believed it was necessary to keep the Law of Moses. Apparently all the rest, or most of the Pharisees, including Paul, didn't think it was necessary to keep the 'Law of Moses', which was the same law that Jesus instructed us to keep in Matthew 5:17-20.

In Acts 21, Paul is meeting with some of the Apostles including James, in Jerusalem, and Paul is accused of being lawless and teaching lawlessness. Acts

21:20-21, **"And when they heard it, they glorified YHVH. And they said to him, "You see, brother, how many myriads of Jews there are who have believed** *(in Jesus)*, **and they are all zealous for the law; 21 but they have been informed about you that you teach all the Jews who are among the Gentiles to forsake Moses, saying that they ought not to circumcise their children nor to walk according to the customs."** The Apostles are telling Paul about their converts in Jerusalem who are '**zealous for the law'**. And then Jesus' own brother, James, inquires about the reports that Paul is teaching his converts that it is OK to forsake Moses' law.

Yes, Paul spoke much about the law being 'done away with' (2Corithians 3:6-17), but he also a number of times express support for the law, saying that it was 'just, holy and good', etc. How do we understand this contradiction in Paul's words? We have to remember that Jesus said that he the Pharisees (including Paul) were 'lawless hypocrite' and Paul was often accused of being a liar, which he denied, even though acknowledged that he lied to 'further the Gospel' (Romans 3:7). So being a hypocritical lawless liar, Paul spoke whatever he needed to say at the time. So, there were times he needed to speak in favor of the keeping the law, in order to have the respect and support of the leaders in the Church. And that's when he spoke about our need to keep God's law. But those few times were offset by his 36 reasons he said that don't need to keep God's law.

Paul was obviously not among the sect of the Pharisees that believed that it was necessary to keep YHVH's law given by Moses. Paul argued against the idea that it was necessary to keep YHVH's law. Why did Paul and most of the Pharisees think it wasn't necessary to keep YHVH's law?

## WHY WERE PAUL AND MOST OF THE PHARISEES LAWLESS?

The Pharisees were a group of religious Jews, who at Jesus' time, felt that salvation had nothing to do with keeping the law of God, but rather salvation was a matter of their national 'election'. Election is the idea that, because of YHVH's promises to Abraham, that all of Abraham's descendants, that's the entire Jewish nation of Israel are YHVH's chosen people, and thus they will all receive YHVH's 'saving grace' simply because they were the chosen, or favored by God – because of Abraham's faith. That means, according to the lawless Pharisees, that the Jews could live in violation of the Commandments of God and still be in YHVH'S future Kingdom because they were physical descendants of Abraham, i.e., Abraham's seed, YHVH's elected or 'chosen', or His 'favored' people. Paul wrote, "**Our Election is not by the law but by promise**" (Galatians 3:17-18).

However, John the Baptizer, who was revered by Jesus as the greatest of the Prophets (Matthew 11:11), spoke YHVH's words to the Pharisees and Sadducees, he said (Matthew 3:8-10, Luke 3:7-9), "**Therefore bear fruits** worthy of repentance, and do not think to say to yourselves, 'We have Abraham as our father.' For I say to you that God is able to rise up children to Abraham from these stones. And even now the ax is laid to the root of the trees. Therefore every tree which does not bear good fruit is cut down and thrown into the fire."** The Pharisees and Sadducees felt that they were automatically saved because they were YHVH's favored (chosen) people, being Abraham's decedents, and that, they believed, made them the 'elect of God'. They felt they were saved by God's promise and God cannot go back on His promise, **"for God's gifts and his call are irrevocable"**. (Romans 11:29) even if they fell into sin. And they reasoned, since they were already 'chosen' by God, it was unnecessary for them to keep the law to obtaining righteousness, or to gain YHVH's saving grace, or to even prove that they were worthy to enter YHVH's kingdom. But, John the Baptizer told them that it doesn't work that way. John said, 'it doesn't matter that you are Abraham's natural seed, because apart from your own 'righteousness' (the fruit of repentance) you will be 'cut down and thrown into the fire'. John and Jesus both agree that they must be willing to submit to YHVH's divine authority to have the righteousness needed be fit for the Kingdom of God. Jesus said in his sermon (Matthew 5:19-20), **"Whoever therefore breaks one of the least of these commandments, and teaches men so, shall be called least in the kingdom of heaven; but whoever does and teaches them, he shall be called great in the kingdom of heaven. 20 For I say to you, that unless your righteousness exceeds the righteousness of the scribes and Pharisees, you will by no means enter the kingdom of heaven"**.

Because of the Pharisee's belief that they were saved because they were the choose people, Abraham's physical seed, it was radical for John the Baptizer and Jesus to preach, **'Repent for the Kingdom of God is at hand'** (Matthew 3:2, 4:17) to the Jews. For many of the Jews, including the Pharisees, believed they were saved by being one of God's elect people they didn't understand why they needed to repent. But, for the humble Jews and the non-Jew among them who acknowledged their sin, and thought they weren't fit for the Kingdom of heaven because they didn't live up to God's standard, or the religious leader's artificial standards, it was great news that they would still be accepted if they would repent and submit to YHVH God's Divine authority– not the authority of the religious leaders. And this we see played out by the story, or parable, of the Publican and the Pharisee (Luke 18).

In Luke 18 Jesus tells us the story of a Publican and a Pharisee both going to the Temple to pray. The Pharisee didn't feel the need to repent, figuring that he was one of God's chosen and he was not under the law (as many Christians do), so sins won't affect where he spends eternity. Of course, they were both sinners, but only the Publican acknowledged his sin and sought forgiveness. The Publican humbled himself before God and asked for God's mercy. Jesus said, of the two, only the Publican went home forgiven (justified) before God.

Jesus told the Scribes and the Pharisees that if they didn't repent they'd be **'cut down and thrown into the fire'**, and we know from Jesus' words, that being 'cut down and thrown into the fire' is the punishment for those who practice lawlessness. In Matthew 13:41-42 Jesus tells us that at Judgment time, it is those who 'practiced lawlessness' that will to be gathered and cast into the furnace of fire – with no exception made for Abraham's decedents, believers in Jesus, those who said the 'sinner's prayer', who pleaded the blood, cling to the cross, been baptized, or for those who were professing Christian or Jews. Fire is the destination for all those who 'practice lawlessness', because God will not have those who spurn His Divine authority in His eternal kingdom.

The Pharisees were considered 'lawless' by Jesus (Matthews 23:28) because they ignored, rejected or set aside some of YHVH's laws (Mark 7:7-9), so they lacked the righteousness needed to enter the Kingdom of God (Matthew 5:19-20). According to Jesus (Matthew 5:17-20), keeping YHVH's Old Testament 'law and the Prophets' until heaven and earth passes away, and repenting when we fail, is the means of gaining the righteousness we need to enter the Kingdom of God, and the Pharisees didn't do that, so they lacked that necessary righteousness. However, true repentance would restore them and all who fall short. They didn't **'do justice, love mercy and walk humbly with their God'** (Micah 6:8) – they didn't think it was necessary.

Paul was clearly among the Pharisees, who believed that they were the elect of God, and then keeping the commandments of God may be a source of blessings, but it does not affect their salvation. Romans 8:33, **"Who shall bring a charge against God's elect? It is God who justifies."** Paul insisted that because they are the 'elect of God', they are already justified by God. And he goes on to say since they are the elect of God, they are saved by grace.

Paul said in Romans 11:5-6, **"Even so then, at this present time there is a remnant according to the election of grace. 6 And if by grace, then it is no longer of works; otherwise grace is no longer grace. But if it is of works, it is no longer grace; otherwise work is no longer work."** According to Paul, people were saved by 'election of grace', and keeping YHVH's law had nothing whatsoever to do with their salvation. According to Paul you can't be saved by keeping the law and you can't be lost by sinning. Romans 8:39, **"nor height nor depth, nor any other created thing, shall be able to separate us from the love of God which is in Christ Jesus our Lord."** Romans 10:9, **"that if you confess with your mouth the Lord Jesus and believe in your heart that God has raised Him from the dead, you will be saved."** According to Paul, we are saved, i.e., grafted into the elect by what we 'confess' and what we 'believe'. And thus according to Paul, salvation is by grace through 'faith' (Ephesians 2:8-9) and for Paul; faith has nothing to do with the law – 'faith' for Paul is the mental accepting of facts – and, according to Paul, by our 'belief' in those facts' we are grafted into YHVH's elect people. And once we are one of the elect, we are automatically saved because of God's promise to Abraham.

For Paul, the law is a non-issue, a person can be saved and still be completely lawless. So according to Paul, a person could be a lawless presumptuous sinner, and still be saved – even though Jesus said that such a person will be cast into a furnace of fire.

On doing an internet search I found 16 reasons why we are 'free from the law' and all sixteen were from Paul's epistles. What does it mean to be 'free from the law'? It simply means that we can ignore, reject, or spurn YHVH's Divine authority and He doesn't care. And if we're spurning His Divine authority it's because we are submitting to another authority that gives is permission to ignore YHVH's Divine authority and Jesus' authority. In other words, we have another god, an authority we have placed over God's authority and that is idolatry, and YHVH does care about that. Jesus, speaking YHVH's words with YHVH's Divine authority said no idolater will enter the Kingdom of God.

Thus Paul was lawless, and he practiced lawlessness, and he trained his Christian converts to be lawless as he was. And, of course, Paul's New Testament letters reflect his thinking, and it's not that he approves of lawlessness, but he doesn't consider it to be a deciding factor in salvation. – And so Paul is simply teaching what the lawless Pharisees believed. That's why Jesus warned us about the teachings of the Pharisees. Matthew 16:12 (NKJV), **"Then they understood that He did not tell them to beware of the leaven of bread, but of the doctrine of the Pharisees and Sadducees."** And Paul boasted about being a Pharisee. Philippians 3:5, **"circumcised the eighth day, of the stock of Israel, of the tribe of Benjamin, a Hebrew of the Hebrews; concerning the law, a Pharisee"**.

As a proud Pharisee, Paul believed that he was above YHVH's law and he would not be charged by God or anyone else with law breaking because he was one of 'YHVH's elect'. Romans 8:33, **"Who shall bring a charge against YHVH's elect? It is God who justifies."** Paul felt that way because he, as Abraham's seed, was selected to be among the 'elect of God' before he did 'any good or evil' – so doing 'good or evil' doesn't affect his being the 'elect' of God. Romans 9:11, **"for the children not yet being born, nor having done any good or evil, that the purpose of God according to election might stand, not of works but of Him who calls."** Abraham was 'elected' solely by YHVH's grace, Romans 11:5, **"Even so then, at this present time there is a remnant according to the election of grace."** And God will never take that election away, according to Paul. Paul insisted that God promised to save 'the elect' and He cannot revoke the promise – even if a person is lawless. Romans 11:29-32, **"For the gifts and the calling of God are irrevocable. 30 For as you were once disobedient to God, yet have now obtained mercy through their** disobedience, 31 even so these also have now been disobedient, that through the mercy shown you they also may obtain mercy. 32 For God has committed them all to disobedience, that He might have mercy on all." According to Paul, disobedience to YHVH's law doesn't disqualify you from being among the saved elect because he understood YHVH's promise to be unconditional, and therefore it cannot be revoked. According to Paul, it's even better if you are disobedient, because then a person must be counting on, and relying on the mercy and grace of God instead of their own works. But Jesus said, 'if you endure in the faith until the end you will be saved', and for Jesus true faith includes doing what God has commanded.

1Thessalonians 1:4, "**knowing, beloved brethren, your election by God.**" National election is the cornerstone of Paul's messages. Paul tells the Thessalonians that they are the 'elect of God'. That is, they are already heirs to the kingdom by their election, so they don't need to keep YHVH's law or do anything else – just believe it. What Paul leaves out of his theory on salvation is our response to God's Divine authority. God has made commands of us, so, is it OK to spurn His authority, and reject or ignore what He said? Will God understand and still consider that person to be one of His 'elect' people? Even if they 'will not submit to His Divine authority'? Perhaps the greater question is; was YHVH's promise to Abraham's physical seed as Paul suggested, or with Abraham's spiritual seed? Paul believed it what the physical seed, and Gentiles could be grafted in (Romans 11).

This is why Paul, when writing to the 'saints' in Colosse, (Colossians chapter 2) Paul tells them that since believers in Jesus are part of that elect, i.e., 'saints' and thus automatically saved. And so they don't have to worry about judgment for violating the law, because symbolically, the penalty for breaking the law was nailed to the cross, "**having wiped out the handwriting of requirements that was against us, which was contrary to us. And He has taken it out of the way, having nailed it to the cross**" (Collusions 2:14). Again, there is no condemnation for the 'Elect' (Romans 8:33) so there is no need to keep God's laws or regulations, so we mustn't let "**no one judge you in food or in drink, or regarding a festival or a new moon or sabbaths**" (Colossians 2:16). It's because, according to Paul's way of thinking, by our 'faith in Christ' we are 'one with him', and therefore among the 'Elect', and there is no condemnation for the 'Elect' regardless of our sins.

## PAUL'S IDEA FOR SALVATION

Everyone knows that Paul wrote in his epistles that we don't need to keep God's law, we are free from it and we will not be condemned for breaking it. And everybody loves that message. However, not everybody knows what he bases that theory on. He bases it on us receiving God grace on account of 'national election' for the Jews and through trusting in Jesus for the non-Jew.

Since Paul believed that all of the Jews will be saved because they are the 'elect of God', being descendants of Abraham, Paul reasoned that if Gentiles are grafted into Israel (Romans 11), then they too will be saved, regardless of any law keeping. Paul figures that if they 'believed in Jesus' and 'confessed him as lord' they would be saved. But, do lawless Gentiles really become one of God's elect? If Jesus was really their lord, wouldn't they obey all he said, like keeping YHVH's "law and Prophets" (Matthew 5:18-19) and worship YHVH alone (Matthew 4:10)?

So clearly the Pharisees didn't feel it was necessary to keep YHVH's 'law and the Prophets' to be saved. And so, that is what Paul believed and taught, so now the entire Christian Church, and they are now like the Pharisees in believing that very same thing. And Jesus called the Pharisee 'lawless hypocrites'. Couldn't the same thing be said about Christian who profess to be God's people, followers of Jesus, and practicing the Christian religion by going to church every Sunday, but don't keep YHVH God's laws and ignore His Prophets. Sounds like 'lawless hypocrites'.

## WHY WAS THE PHARISEES' WORSHIP IN VAIN?

Mathew 15:7-9 (NKJV), "**Hypocrites! Well did Isaiah prophesy about you, saying: 8 'These people draw near to Me with their mouth, And honor Me with their lips, But their heart is far from Me. 9 And in vain they worship Me, Teaching as doctrines the commandments of men.'** "

Mark 7:7-8, "**And in vain they worship Me, teaching as doctrines the commandments of men.' 8 For laying aside the commandment of God, you hold the tradition of men—the washing of pitchers and cups, and many other such things you do."**

The Pharisees were known for the fastidious law keeping. To call someone a 'Pharisee' today is to fault them for paying too close attention to legal details of the law, as the Pharisees did. The Pharisees did keep the 'law', but the wrong law. In addition to the Law of Moses, the Pharisees had another law, called the 'oral law', which was the 'traditions of man', or 'doctrines of man'. The Rabbis claim that the 'Oral laws' was also from God, and they consider it the most important part of the God's revelation to mankind, even though the Scriptures don't even mention the 'Oral law'.

The Pharisee, like Christians, lightly esteemed YHVH's law and the Prophets. They would sometimes neglect YHVH's law and the Prophets. So the Pharisees had no problem with setting aside some of YHVH's laws to keep their 'Oral laws' (Traditions) and they felt justified in doing that, for they were told, by their passed down traditions, that the oral law supersedes the written law. They too were deceived. Jesus tried to convince them that the written law supersedes the oral law, but they violently opposed his message. God was not pleased with their neglecting the written law for the oral law, and Jesus let them know.

Jesus had this interesting exchange with a rich young ruler; Matthew 19:17-19 (NKJV), **"Why do you ask me about what is good?" Jesus replied. "There is only One who is good. If you want to enter life, keep the commandments."**
**18 "Which ones?" he inquired. Jesus replied, "'You shall not murder, you shall not commit adultery, you shall not steal, you shall not give false testimony, 19 honor your father and mother,' and 'love your neighbor as yourself.'** Jesus told the rich young ruler to keep the commandments if he wanted eternal life, to which the rich young ruler asked, 'Which one?" At first blush we must consider that to be a strange question, since being a Jewish ruler, he knew the Ten Commandments, as well as the rest of YHVH's Torah law. So why did he ask, "Which ones?" He asked that because when Jesus said keep the 'Commandment' he wasn't sure if Jesus was referring to the Jewish 'Oral law' as the Pharisees probably told him, or YHVH's written Torah law as given by Moses. (We can't keep them both for there are conflicts between them. That's what Jesus was referring to when he said trying to put new wine in an old wine skin will ruin them both.) In responding to the ruler's question, Jesus then started quoting the Ten Commandments, and before Jesus was done with them, the rich young ruler got his answer. It's not the 'Oral law' which gives eternal life, but rather it's YHVH's written Torah law. Seemingly it's OK to keep the 'Oral law' but when keeping it conflicts with YHVH's Torah law, the 'Oral law' must be discarded. We must submit to YHVH's Torah law, which is an expression of His Divine authority.

Also note, in this passage in verse 17, Jesus said he was not good, only God was good. This is a denial that Jesus is God. The Greek word for 'good' here means perfect without flaw. Jesus said he wasn't perfect, but God was.

## DO WE WORSHIP IN VAIN?

Jesus said the Pharisees' worship of YHVH was in vain (Mark 7:7-8) because they were practicing lawlessness, that is, they set aside some of the commandments of God to keep their traditions (Oral laws). And having set aside some of YHVH's laws, they violated them, and didn't even consider it to be a sin and thus never they repented and that makes them lawless. Lawless people are that way because they have accepted some 'lawless' religious authority which told them that it was OK to set aside some of YHVH's commandments to keep their traditions instead, and then they spurned YHVH's Divine authority to keep those oral traditions. And we can't worship a God we dishonor by our disobedience, apart from true repentance.

The Pharisees listened to their god (supreme authority) and ignored YHVH God. Their disobedience to YHVH's commands made it clear that YHVH God was not their supreme authority, and therefore He was not their true god. And YHVH God will not accept worship from those who dishonor Him by spurning His Divine authority as expressed in His laws and commandments. Doesn't that sounds like today's Christian Church, following religious traditions, doctrines and creeds instead of Jesus' instructions, and YHVH's law and the Prophets which they lightly esteem?

The Christian Church today knows YHVH's 'law and the Prophets', but they reject them and enjoy their Easter Sunday Ham dinners. They reject YHVH's Sabbath command and keep Sunday instead of His Sabbath day, they reject YHVH's dietary laws and eat pig, and keep the Pagan fertility feast day of Easter, with its Easter eggs and Easter bunny, instead of YHVH's Passover which God commanded us to observe for all generations (Exodus 12:14). And even worse, they reject the First Commandment which commands us to worship YHVH alone (Exodus 20:2-3) and instead they abide by their man made Nicene Creed so they worship Jesus and the Trinity. And do they feel guilt, shame, godly sorrow or do they repent for doing these things? No, they don't even consider what they do as sin because they have been deceived by the Christian Church and they have unknowing joined Babylon the Great and they unwittingly worship the Beast or his image.

The Christian Church is as lawless and the Pharisees were, and Jesus said unless our righteousness exceeds that of the Pharisees we will not be allowed into the Kingdom of God. (Matthew 5:20). I believe that if Jesus spoke that today he would have said, 'if your righteousness doesn't exceed that of the Orthodox Jews and the Christians, we will not be allowed into the Kingdom of God.'

So, no, YHVH God will not accept the worship of those in the Christian Church, because they all commit idolatry by worship the Trinity instead of YHVH God. And, no, YHVH is not part of the Trinity for He told us He is the only true God and will not share His glory, worship or praise with other gods, for He is a Jealous God and He will be a consuming fire those who practice idolatry. Isaiah 44:6, "**Thus says YHVH, the King of Israel, And his Redeemer, YHVH of hosts: 'I am the First and I am the Last; Besides Me there is no god".**

## WAS PAUL AN APOSTATE?

I made the charges that Paul was lawless, but I'm not the only one saying that. In Acts 21:21(YLT) we read that James confronted Paul, "**and they are instructed concerning thee, that apostasy from Moses thou dost teach to all Jews among the nations, saying -- Not to circumcise the children, nor**

**after the customs to walk".** James, Jesus' brother, and the leader of the young Messianic movement, said that Paul had apostatized from the Law of Moses'.

Paul, being a Pharisee, reflected the idea that the Jews are the 'elect of God' and thus God will save His elect (Romans 8:33, 9:11, 11:5, Colossians 3:12, 1Thessalonians 1:4, etc.), and that election is an "election of grace". And that thinking is reflected in Paul's New Testament writings. For Paul "election of grace" had nothing to do with YHVH's law, and thus he said salvation is by 'grace' apart from the law because, as he reasoned, Abraham and the Hebrews were chosen by God before the law was given, so the law was not a factor in the promise. Paul said that it was by faith in Jesus, apart from the law that results in us being grafted into the 'elect' people of Israel (Romans 11, Ephesians 2). And according to Paul, you could have a true faith in Jesus and not obey him, and you could have a true faith in God and not obey Him and still be saved because of that national election.

And while it is true that Abraham died before the law of Moses was given, but yet, God had commands that He gave to Abraham. And we read in Genesis 26:5 (NKJV), **"because Abraham obeyed My voice and kept My charge, My commandments, My statutes, and My laws".** Abraham submitted to YHVH's Divine authority.

Paul wrote; **"Salvation is by grace through faith apart from the law"** (Ephesians 2:8-9). **"If you confess Jesus is lord and believe in your heart the God raised him from the dead you are saved"** (Romans 10:9-10). **"Nothing can separate us from the love of God"** (Romans 8:35-39). **'Righteousness by faith apart from the law'** (Romans 3:21). And another catchall phrase that falsely assures lawless and rebellious sinners that they will get into YHVH's eternal kingdom, **"There is no condemnation for those in Christ Jesus"** (Romans 8:1). According to this way of thinking, a person can go ahead and sin like the devil and still be saved if they are one of the 'elect'. That's the dangerous Pharisee's teaching that Jesus warned us about.

Peter also warned us of Paul's teachings, in 2Peter 3:14-16, Peter tells us that if we understand Paul to be saying that we can be 'lawless' (ignoring YHVH's Old Testament law) and still be saved (because of national election), we have misunderstood him to our own destruction. And the Apostle John warns us about not abiding in the teachings of Jesus (2John 9-10), that is, we mustn't forsake what Jesus said just to follow what Paul said. However, that is the very thing the Christian Church has done, and is still doing.

Jesus disagreed that salvation is by national election apart from YHVH's law. John 8:39, **"They answered and said to Him, "Abraham is our father." Jesus said to them, "If you were Abraham's children, you would do the works of Abraham."** Jesus said the election is for Abraham's spiritual seed, those who submit to YHVH's Divine authority, not his physical seed. Keeping Jesus' words, or the Everlasting Gospel, will make us Abraham's spiritual seed.

Jesus said salvation happens by keeping his word (John 8:51, 10:27-28, Matthew 7:24-25). Does being 'chosen' or 'elect' mean you don't have to obey YHVH's laws? Can we be one of YHVH's elect and reject what God said, and reject what Jesus said? Can we even think that one of YHVH's elect could reject YHVH's and Jesus' authorities, despise their words, and submit to some other lawless authority instead? No. YHVH's elect don't defiantly look His in the eye and say, 'No, I won't'. Isaiah 56:1-5 and other passages tell us that we will be one of YHVH's elect, one of His choose people, when we submit to His Divine authority and keep His covenant commandments.

## PAUL'S TEACHINGS IN CONTRAST TO JESUS' TEACHINGS

Paul's lawless teachings are completely contrary to what Jesus taught. Jesus said, for one to enter the kingdom of God we must keep the commandments of God (Matthew 5:17-20, 7:24-25, 19:17, Mark 10:18-19, Luke 18:18-20, Revelation 12:17, 14:12, 22:14 and others). And it's not that we are saved by a mechanical obedience, but rather obedience is evidence of our saving relationship with God (John 14:15,21, 23-24), and it's a submissive and obedient character which is the type of character that God wants in His eternal kingdom (Micah 6:8) – and that's how we become the truly elect of God. Those who obey God demonstrate their love, honor, respect, reverence, faith, and the fear of God. Jesus and Moses both said God loves those who love Him and keeps His commandments (John 14:21-24, Exodus 20:6, Isaiah 56:1-6) and God will give His saving grace to those whom He loves.

Those who keep YHVH's commandments demonstrate their faith and love by their willingness to submit to His Divine authority. While those who reject, set aside or ignore YHVH's Old Testament laws, 'practice lawlessness', and in doing that they show a lack of love, honor, respect, reverence, faith or fear of God, they are in rebellion against YHVH's Divine authority, despising His word (Number 15:31) and thereby they are dishonoring Him by not doing His will. Those who reject YHVH's laws have a different supreme authority, a lawless authority, and therefore YHVH God is not their true god, and their worship of Him is in vain, and their prayers are not even heard (Proverbs 28:9).

So, can a person reject YHVH's Sabbath day, eat pork, and reject YHVH's Passover, worship the Trinity, enjoy Easter Sunday Ham Dinners and still be saved? Who is saved and who is not saved is up to God, but from what I read in the Scriptures, those who know YHVH's laws and His will, and yet do not keep them are in trouble. Hebrews 5:9 (NKJV), "**and, once made perfect, he became the source of eternal salvation for all who obey him** ". Hebrews

10:26 (NKJV), **"For if we sin willfully after we have received the knowledge of the truth, there no longer remains a sacrifice for sins."** That is, there is no atonement possible, not even Jesus' blood, for those who know God's law, i.e., His will, and presumptuously violate it anyway. And if there is no atonement, their sins are still on their record at judgment time. If we know that God forbids something and we do it anyway, there will be no forgiveness or atonement apart from true repentance. Please don't ever eat an Easter Sunday Ham dinner – if you do, or have in the past, ask God to forgive you and vow never to do it again. If I were to re-write Matthew 7:21, **"Not every Christian who calls Jesus, 'Lord,' shall enter the kingdom of heaven, but only the ones who have submitted to YHVH's Divine authority**."

Paul's lawless message is taught and preached by those who the Scriptures refer to as false prophets (pastors, priests, ministers, teachers, etc.).

## WHO ARE THESE FALSE PROPHETS?

According to Jesus (Matthew 7:15-23) false prophets come to us wearing sheep's clothing. Who wears sheep's clothing? The ancient shepherds all wore "sheep's clothing". Who are the shepherds of God's flock today? It's the pastors, priests, and teachers who claim to represent Christ but they preach and teach lawlessness. The false prophets (pastors, priest and teachers) are not evil, nor do they have evil intents, for they themselves are deceived and have accepted Paul's lawless teachings, and they teach it and preach it, causing people to practice lawlessness. While they believe they are doing YHVH's work, they have unwittingly and unknowingly become the 'false prophets' whom Jesus spoke about; Matthew 23:11-12 (NKJV), **"Then many false prophets will rise up and deceive many. 12 And because lawlessness will abound, the love of many will grow cold**." Those who teach and preach Paul's brand of lawlessness are teaching that we don't need to keep YHVH's Old Testament law, and they support that idea using one or more of Paul's 36 reasons why we don't need to keep YHVH's law. That also makes Paul a false prophet.

Lamentation 2:14a, **"Your prophets have seen for you false and deceptive visions; they have not uncovered your iniquity,"** They do not point out the peoples sins, nor do they call on them to repent. Jeremiah 5:31, **"The prophets prophesy falsely, and the priests rule by their own power; and My people love to have it so. But what will you do in the end?"** Jeremiah warns us that the false prophets give messages that people love to hear, like "you don't need to keep YHVH's laws", and God loves you so much that he'd never condemn you, and 'for there is no condemnation for those who believe in Christ Jesus'. Just believe in Jesus, cling to the cross, plead the blood, say the sinner's prayer, be baptized, receive communion, go to confession, pray to Mary, pray to Jesus, pray to the Saints, etc.

Jeremiah 14:14, YHVH says the false prophets come in My name and speak words I didn't tell them to speak.

### THE EARLY CHURCH WASN'T LAWLESS

Acts 24:14, **"But this I confess to you, that according to the Way which they call a sect, so I worship the God of my fathers, believing all things which are written in the Law and in the Prophets."** The early Church led by Jesus' apostles and his personal disciples, kept YHVH's Old Testament 'law and the Prophets' and they worshiped YHVH alone. They weren't lawless, and they didn't eat pork, celebrate Easter, nor did they worship Jesus or the Trinity. They were Bible believing Jews who keep YHVH's law and believed that Jesus was YHVH's anointed messiah and worshiped YHVH alone. The early church did not accept Paul's lawless message – only later was it included in the Bible. The early church was practicing Biblical Judaism – and it did until they embraced Paul's teachings, and accepted the Trinity.

### BY FOLLOWING PAUL'S TEACHINGS WE BECOME LAWLESS

Most Christians today see no problem with eating Easter Sunday Ham dinners, rejecting God's Sabbath, worshiping the Trinity, or abortion, which God would call an abomination. And, no, Jesus did not OK the eating of ham; he said we are to keep every jot and tittle of the law. He did say that all food was ceremonial clean (Mark 7:19), saying that all kosher food is ceremonially clean, and ham wasn't considered to be a food. Decades later, in Acts 10, Peter says he had still never eaten anything unclean. Peter obviously didn't think Jesus OK'ing the eating of unclean foods. Jesus never would have done that, for that would have been a violation of YHVH's laws, making Jesus a law breaker, and despising YHVH's words. Also, even if Jesus had said that, the disciples and Apostles would never accept a man's authority over YHVH's authority. So they would have rejected Jesus' canceling out one of YHVH's commands. They would have regarded him as a false prophet.

When Christianity has no problem doing what God considers to be an abomination, they have lost their moral compass. They practice lawlessness, forsaken God's laws – while being religious at the same time, going to church every Sunday and singing their Christian hymns. And we can thank Paul for that because he said we didn't need to be righteous on our own. According to Paul, we will not be judged according to our own righteousness, but according to Jesus' righteousness, he tells us that we will have Jesus' righteousness imputing into us before the Judgment. Paul needed to invent the idea of "imputed righteous" to compensate for the 'totally depraved' idea that he also invented. According to Paul we have no ability to be righteous on our own, so we need Jesus to be righteous for us.

Paul, while trying to prove 'total depravity' misquotes the Old Testament (Psalm 14) when he said 'there are none righteous, no not one' – he ripped it out context. In Psalm 14, said that, but it was referring to '**fools who say there is no god**'. And we do read that there many people in the Scriptures who are called 'righteous': Abraham (Genesis 15:6), Job (Job 32:1), King David (Psalm 18:20), King Asa (1Kings 15:11), King Hezekiah (2 King. 18:3), King Josiah (2 King. 22:1-2), Enoch (Hebrew 11:5), Moses (Deut.18:13), Abel and Zacharias (Matthew 23:35), Joseph, Mary's husband (Matthew 1:19), Joseph, the counsellor (Luke 23:50), Cornelius (Acts 10:1 – 2), John the Baptist (Mark 6:20), Simeon (Luke 2:25), the priest Zacharias and his wife Elisabeth (Luke 1:6). Plus there are many verses which speak about plight and trials of 'righteous' people. Contrary to what Paul said, John said, **"he who practices righteousness is righteous, just as He is righteous."**

In John 5:24-30 Jesus tells us that he will judge us according to our doing the 'Father's will'. In Matthew 7:22-23 those who didn't do 'the Father's will' were condemned for 'practicing lawlessness'. So clearly it is God's will that we submit to His Divine authority, i.e., obeying all He said. In Matthew 13:41-42 Jesus said those who practice lawlessness, at the end of time, will be gathered and cast into a fiery furnace.

## WAS PAUL REBUKED BY THE TRUE APOSTLES?

Because of the order the in which New Testament book are placed in the Bible, one might think that the Gospels were written first, emphasizing the Old Testament law, and then Paul's letters came later to explain a new way of salvation, by grace apart from the law, i.e., the New Covenant. But that's not true at all. Paul's letters were written first, and then years later, perhaps in response to Paul's letters, the Apostles wrote the Gospels, and the Apostolic epistles. If you study the Gospels, along with James and John's letters, it seems like they were writing to correct Paul's theology.

Paul wrote that Jesus came in the "likeness" or "appearance" of "sinful human flesh", also Phil 2:7, "appeared to be a man". Paul calls Jesus a 'life giving spirit', 1 Corinthians 15:45, – but John wrote, that's 'not true', he was totally human, we saw him and we touched him (1John 1:1-3 and also in Acts 2:22 Peter refers to Jesus as a man). Paul wrote that the Law passed away, Matthew quoted Jesus as saying that the Law won't pass away until heaven and earth pass away (Matthew 5:17-19). Paul said twice it was OK to eat meat sacrificed to idols (1Corth 8:4, 10:28), John records that Jesus said 'No' to that twice in the Book of Revelations (2:12, 2:20) and called on them to repent. Paul said that "good works" (i.e., obedience to YHVH's law) are not necessary; only an academic faith is needed to be saved. James, Jesus' half-brother, said, 'No, Paul, good works are needed for salvation; faith without good works is dead'. Paul argues that we are robed with Christ's righteousness; Jesus in the Book of Revelation tells us that the 'Bride' prepares herself for the wedding, and her white linen robe is the "righteous acts of the saints". And John tells us do not be deceived, he who does righteousness is righteous (1John 3:7). Paul tells us that we are 'totally depraved' therefore we can't overcome sin on our own, but Jesus calls on us to repent and choose righteousness. Jesus said the righteousness we need to enter the kingdom of God comes from our submission to YHVH's Divine authority as found in his law and the Prophets (Matthew 5:18-20), but Paul said righteousness comes to us by what we believe. Paul included predestination in his theology, as though we are not in charge of our destiny, yet the rest of the Scriptures clearly tell us that we have a free choice – we may choose life or death. Paul said sin doesn't stop us from receiving YHVH's saving grace since it comes by faith alone, but Jude 4 says that is turning the grace of God into a license to sin. Paul either was ignorant of Jesus' teachings or was a liar. Peter wrote that if we understand Paul to be saying that we can be lawless and still be saved, we have a wrong understanding of Paul's words. In other words, he couldn't believe that Paul would say such a thing. But he did.

Paul bragged the he was a first class Pharisee, Philippians 3:5, and then the Gospel of Matthew (Matthew 16:12) reports that Jesus warns us about the teachings of the Pharisees and he referred to the Pharisees as lawless hypocrites (Matthew 23:28). In the parable of the Wheat and the Tares (Matthew 13:24-43), Jesus tells us that a bad 'seed' of 'lawlessness' was planted in the Churches, and those who practiced lawlessness will be gathered and cast into a fiery furnace. Who could it be teaching that 'lawlessness', other than Paul through his lawless epistles?

Paul wrote that there is no righteous people (Romans 3:10), yet the Gospels point out, and identify many righteous people: Abel and Zacharias (*Matthew 23:35)*, Joseph, Mary's husband (*Matthew 1:19)*, Joseph, the counsellor (*Luke 23:50)*, Cornelius (*Acts 10:1 – 2)*, John the Baptist (*Mark 6:20)*, Simeon (*Luke 2:25)*, The priest Zacharias and his wife Elisabeth (Luke 1:6).

Paul believed in the Greek dualism, that is, the soul can function outside of the body. He said in 2Corthians 5:8, **"But we are confident, and have a good will to be absent rather from the body, and to be present with the Lord"**. Greek dualism is a belief that on the death of the body, the soul leaves the body and floats to heaven, or hell. Most of Judaism, then and today, believed in a bodily resurrection only, no soul floating to heaven after death, which Paul seemed to believe in. However, Jesus' Apostles were clear in their Gospels that Jesus rose from the dead bodily (John 20:17-20), thus rejecting Paul's teaching of dualism and Jesus being a 'spirit'.

Paul is blunt in telling us that the Law is abolished, done away with, we are not under the law but under grace, it was nailed to a tree, has faded away and was only ordained by angels who are not gods. This Pauline theology leads to practicing lawlessness. And while Paul didn't invent the Trinity, his writings were the building blocks used for that false teaching. Paul, even though he never met Jesus often referred to Jesus and a 'spirit' and didn't seem to understand that Jesus was a man, as the Scriptures tell us, Peter said in Acts 2:22, **"Men of Israel, hear these words: Jesus of Nazareth, a man attested by God to you by miracles, wonders, and signs which God did through Him in your midst, as you yourselves also know".** Jesus was often called a Prophet (Acts 3:22, 7:37, Matthew 21:11, 21:46, Luke 7:16, John 1:21, 4:19, 6:14, etc. and even referred to himself as a prophet (Matthew 13:57, Luke 4:24, 13:33, Mark 6:3-4, John 3:34, 12:49, 14:10, 17:8). Yet, in verses such as; Ephesians 2, Romans 9:5, Titus 2:13, and Colossians 2:9-10 Paul deifies Jesus, and that results in idolatry and is the foundation stone for the Doctrine of the Trinity.

Jesus also referred to himself as 'son of man' or literally, 'son of Adam', in other words identifying himself as a human. Jesus also referred to himself as the 'Son of God' which is a somewhat common term in the Old and New Testament Scriptures. Created beings, such as angels we referred to as 'sons of God', the people of Israel were called the 'sons of God', because YHVH was their Father who begat, created or somehow made them. Being the 'son of God' does not mean a person is God – it means that they were somehow begotten by the Father.

It's like what Peter said; some things Paul wrote are hard to understand. If Paul was indeed saying that we can reject the law of God, according to Peter he was wrong. But did Paul really say that? We do know that's how he is understood by most people and most churches, even though he also wrote some verses about the need to keep YHVH's law. But, one way or another, I will listen to Paul only so long as he conforms to Jesus' teachings because I am a follower of Jesus, and Jesus said that he is to be our only teacher, Matthew 23:8-10. And Jesus told us that we are to go into 'all the world' and teach all of what he commanded us, Matthew 28:20 – that's why I'm writing this book.

## A LYING SPIRIT?

And I realize that Paul claims that he got his teachings from 'the Lord' (Jesus). He did get them from a spirit, but Paul's teachings are too contrary to Jesus' teachings, or YHVH's teachings, so Paul's teachings are not of Divine origins. It was a different spirit that gave him his message. Perhaps God sent him a lying spirit to test people, like He did in 1Kings 22:22-23, **"YHVH said to him, 'In what way?' So he said, 'I will go out and be a lying spirit in the mouth of all his prophets.' And YHVH said, 'You shall persuade him, and also prevail. Go out and do so.' 23 Therefore look! YHVH has put a lying spirit in the mouth of all these prophets of yours, and YHVH has declared disaster against you."**

God not only allowed Adam and Eve to be tested, He orchestrated the test for their benefit. God allowed Satan to test Job. God allowed Satan to test Jesus. It is reasonable to assume that God has provided Paul's lawless message to be our own 'serpent beast's' message for our own 'Adam and Eve' test. The failure of that test is what we need to understand to move us to true repentance.

We read in Deuteronomy 13 that God will allow us to be tempted, and that is for the purpose of testing our love and commitment for Him. Deuteronomy 13:3, "...**you shall not listen to the words of that false prophet or that dreamer of dreams, for YHVH your God is testing you to know whether you love YHVH your God with all your heart and with all your soul**".

So will YHVH God allow temptations to come our way to test us? YHVH God absolutely will allow temptations to come our way, and He will even orchestrate those tests.

### "FAITH OF JESUS" VS. "FAITH IN JESUS"

FAITH OF JESUS - In Revelation 14:12 we hear Jesus say, "**Here is the patience of the saints; here are those who keep the commandments of God and the faith of Jesus.**"

What was the 'faith of Jesus'. Jesus believed and trusted the Old Testament, he was a Bible believing Jew who would not allow manmade laws, rules, religions, or the traditions of man to supersede the Scriptures. For Jesus, the words of the Scriptures were supreme. And Jesus spoke YHVH's words with YHVH's authority, according to Deuteronomy 18:18-19, Acts 3:22, 7:37, and John 14:10, 12:48, The 'Faith of Jesus' is to have faith the words of the Scripture and faith in Jesus' words, that is to believe, trust and obey all he told us. That is taking Jesus' words at face value and doing what he said, regardless of anything he did. He said what he did in the flesh counts for nothing and it's his words that give us eternal life (John 6:63, 68). For those with 'faith of Jesus', they attempt to keep God's Commandments and laws, and so for them, sin is a problem and then true repentance is necessary. Like Jesus, those with the "faith of Jesus" will submit to YHVH's Divine authority.

FAITH IN JESUS - Romans 3:26, "**to demonstrate at the present time His righteousness, that He might be just and the justifier of the one who has faith in Jesus.**" Paul, and only Paul used the phrase, **'faith in Jesus'**.

"Faith in Jesus" is to have faith in the person of Jesus, that is, to believe he is who he said he was and to trust in what he did, rather than what he said. This faith is a focus on John 3:16 without caring to grasp the true understanding of the word 'believe' – "believing" as they understand it, is to mental acceptance of some facts. 'Faith in Jesus' is to focus on his birth, live, death and resurrection. These people aren't too worried about sin, because they believe that Jesus died for their sins, past, present and future sins. So, sin is no big deal as long as they believe that Jesus died for their sins and rose from the dead – so true repentance is not necessary.

Many evil people, who have done bad things have 'faith in Jesus', and regardless of their sins they believe that Jesus is their lord and savior. They are those on the Broad Way sing Christian hymns all the way to their judgment. That is just like the murders on death row talking about their faith in Jesus.

Jesus teaches that salvation is by having the 'faith of Jesus'. However, it's only Paul that teaches and preaches the idea of 'Faith in Jesus'. And of course Paul also teaches and preaches the 36 reasons why we don't need to keep YHVH's laws. For Paul, when we have 'faith in Jesus' we a grafted into Israel as one of God's chosen people, and thus we are justified and saved. For those who believe that they are saved by their 'faith in Jesus' there is no need to keep God's laws, or commandments. For Paul said if you believe in Jesus are saved, having done good or evil (Romans 9:11).

Thus those with 'Faith of Jesus' will submit to YHVH's Divine authority while those with a simply 'faith in Jesus', according to their understanding of salvation, need not submit to YHVH's Divine authority to be saved, In other words, "Faith in Jesus" allows a person to defiantly spurn YHVH's Divine authority, look Him in the eye, and say, 'No, I will not'.- and yet believe themselves to be saved because of Jesus' life, death and resurrection.

Paul never met Jesus and didn't know Jesus. When we see signs that say, "JESUS SAVES" we can understand that that is a Pauline message, from his epistles, which the churches embrace. But, the truth is, Jesus doesn't save us, but he does tell us how to be saved.

## PREDICTED APOSTASY FROM JESUS' TEACHINGS

In the Book of the Revelation Jesus warns us that 'all the world' would be deceived and wonder after the beast (Revelation 12:9, 13:3). While spoken by Jesus it was foreseen as God looking into the future. But even before the Book of the Revelation was written, back in the Gospels, Jesus foresaw this would happen when he said, "**I have come in My Father's name, and you do not receive Me; if another comes in his own name, him you will receive**" (John 5:43). Jesus is referring to Paul here, coming in his own name. The Christian community has reject Jesus' message to worship YHVH alone and to keep YHVH's law and the Prophets, but has received Paul's message to set aside the law of God and His commandments.

## THE BOOK OF THE REVELATION IS ANTI-PAUL

It seems that after all the rest of the New Testament books were written there is still much room for confusion. While Jesus in the Gospels told us to keep YHVH's law and the Prophets, Paul wrote that we didn't need to keep YHVH's law and the Prophets, telling us that we will not be judged for it. Paul tells us that we are free from condemnation if we trust in Jesus, faith in him. That he said will graph us into God's covenant people, and then we are automatically saved, by the grace of election. However the Gospels disagree with that idea, and from them we hear that we need to keep YHVH's law and the Prophets, and our righteous is dependent on that.

So with two opposing views, we need a final arbitrator, to tell us which of those two views are correct. The Arbitrator is YHVH God, as we read that He gave the message to Jesus. The Book of the Revelation is a message from the Arbitrator. The Book of the Revelation is God's last word, and it is another witness against Paul's theology. In addition, through the Seven Churches, which were all founded by Paul, and the Four Horses, we see the effects of those who embrace Paul's theology, and that is the practicing of lawlessness and idolatry. To those in the churches YHVH tells us to get out before the plagues start.

How do we get out of the condemned church? We do that by obeying the Everlasting Gospel, which as we read, is not compatible with today's Christian faith.

## CHAPTER CONCLUSION

Ultimately we have to choose between Paul and Jesus. Paul said that we didn't need to keep God's law and he gave us 36 reasons why and how righteousness comes for our faith apart from the law. The Christian Church as embraced Paul's epistles. Hook, line and sinker, as though they are Divinely inspired. Yet, Jesus told us to keep the law and the Prophets, every jot and tittle, until heaven and earth pass away. Their words are so contrary that we can't keep them both. As Jesus said, we can only have one master, so we must choose between authorities.

Paul bragged about be a Pharisee and Jesus said the Pharisees were 'lawless hypocrites', and we are to beware of their doctrines. Paul shows himself to be a lawless hypocrite.

Paul's words can't be trusted, he is a lawless hypocrite. But, then I ask, do we need his words? Do we need his teachings? Do we need his doctrines? Jesus told us that he is to be our only teacher (Matthew 23:10) and Jesus has the 'words of eternal life' (John 6:68), Jesus also told us that if we kept his words we would receive eternal life (Matthew 7:24-25, John 10:27-28), and if we didn't keep his words we would not receive eternal life (Matthew 7:26-27, John 8:51). Jesus' words are compatible with the Everlasting Gospel. And we can't keep Jesus' words if we are keeping Paul's words, so we need to set Paul's words aside and embrace Jesus' words.

End of Chapter

As a result of their salvation the redeemed Praise YHVH God Almighty.... Revelation 15:3-4, **"They sing the song of Moses, the servant of God, and the song of the Lamb, saying: "Great and marvelous** *are* **Your works, YHVH God Almighty! Just and true** *are* **Your ways, O King of the saints!** *(saints are the subjects of God's kingdom, because they accept God's authority over them, and thus they keep the commandments of God and the Faith of Jesus, Revelation 14:12)*

Revelation 15:4, **"Who shall not <u>fear</u> You, O YHVH and <u>glorify</u> Your name? For** *You* **alone** *are* **holy. For all nations shall come and <u>worship</u> before You, for Your judgments have been manifested."** - *Moses and the Lamb both tell us to worship YHVH God Almighty.*

Those who acknowledge that YHVH alone is God, have the faith of Jesus and they will submit to YHVH Divine authority. Those who accept the Trinity, and (or) Jesus, as God, see no need to keep the commandments because their God died on a cross so they can be free from keeping the commandments and YHVH's laws.

Ecclesiastes 12:13-14 "**Let us hear the conclusion of the whole matter:**
**Fear God and keep His commandments, For this is man's all. For God will bring every work into judgment, Including every secret thing, Whether good or evil."**

Praise YHVH,
Don Werner

Printed in Great Britain
by Amazon